Vietnam War

A Captivating Guide to the Second Indochina War

© **Copyright 2017**

All rights Reserved. No part of this book may be reproduced in any form without permission in writing from the author. Reviewers may quote brief passages in reviews.

Disclaimer: No part of this publication may be reproduced or transmitted in any form or by any means, mechanical or electronic, including photocopying or recording, or by any information storage and retrieval system, or transmitted by email without permission in writing from the publisher.

While all attempts have been made to verify the information provided in this publication, neither the author nor the publisher assumes any responsibility for errors, omissions, or contrary interpretations of the subject matter herein.

This book is for entertainment purposes only. The views expressed are those of the author alone, and should not be taken as expert instruction or commands. The reader is responsible for his or her actions.

Adherence to all applicable laws and regulations, including international, federal, state and local laws governing professional licensing, business practices, advertising, and all other aspects of doing business in the US, Canada, UK, or any other jurisdiction is the sole responsibility of the purchaser or reader.

Neither the author nor the publisher assumes any responsibility or liability whatsoever on behalf of the purchaser or reader of these materials. Any perceived slight of any individual or organization is purely unintentional.

Contents

FREE BONUS FROM CAPTIVATING HISTORY (AVAILABLE FOR A LIMITED TIME) 7

INTRODUCTION 1

CHAPTER 1 – THE FRENCH AND THE FIRST INDOCHINA WAR 3

CHAPTER 2 – OUT OF THE FRYING PAN, INTO THE FIRE: THE GOVERNMENT OF NGO DINH DIEM 16

CHAPTER 3 – PRAGMATISM AND IDEALISM 24

CHAPTER 4 – THE DEATH OF TWO CATHOLIC PRESIDENTS 29

CHAPTER 5 – SMOKE AND MIRRORS: JOHNSON'S WAR 36

CHAPTER 6 – THE AMERICAN WAR MACHINE 44

CHAPTER 7 – THE TET NIGHTMARE 51

CHAPTER 8 – NIXON AND KISSINGER 57

CONCLUSION 70

PREVIEW OF WORLD WAR 2 .... **73**

A CAPTIVATING GUIDE FROM BEGINNING TO END **73**

FREE BONUS FROM CAPTIVATING HISTORY (AVAILABLE FOR A LIMITED TIME) **87**

SOURCES **88**

Free Bonus from Captivating History (Available for a Limited time)

Hi History Lovers!

Now you have a chance to join our exclusive history list so you can get your first history ebook for free as well as discounts and a potential to get more history books for free! Simply visit the link below to join.

Captivatinghistory.com/ebook

Also, make sure to follow us on:

Twitter: @Captivhistory

Facebook: Captivating History: @captivatinghistory

Introduction

The Vietnam War represented a watershed not only in American and Vietnamese history but also internationally. It wasn't just a battle between two nations, but between two ideologies, two military strategies and a fight for the hearts and minds of two vastly different national populations.

To the Americans, it represented young American men defending the democratic rights of a foreign population against a dangerous and corrupting ideology. To the North Vietnamese, it represented their nationalist struggle to unify their country which had been repressed by colonialism, then divided by another foreign power.

Henry Kissinger would say in 1969, "I refuse to believe that a fourth-rate power like North Vietnam doesn't have a breaking point." Despite being committed to Vietnam since 1945, the American government failed to understand the nature of the war they were involved in 24 years later. This sums up American involvement in Vietnam. The broad-brush strokes of the American military couldn't translate to the painting of Vietnam, which required finer details.

The Vietnamese were used to fighting foreign enemies long before U.S. troops arrived in Danang. Vietnamese nationalism had germinated under foreign occupation since 40 A.D. The idea of fighting an unlimited war with every drop of blood and scrap of resource the population could give was not alien to the Vietnamese, a concept which the American government could not understand.

Few conflicts in global history symbolise as much as Vietnam. From the civil rights movement to the role of the media in warfare, the Vietnam War was unique in the sense that it could not be contained as a military matter but transcended across every area of Vietnamese and American society. The word 'Vietnam' describes an era of history, not just an isolated war in a small nation in Southeast Asia. It is the lens through which the America and Vietnam of today must be interpreted. Few conflicts have or will ever shape the world as much as the Vietnam War.

Chapter 1 – The French and the First Indochina War

The history of Vietnam is a history of occupiers, emancipation and a national struggle. From 1428 when the Vietnamese secured their independence from their Chinese occupiers, until the Vietnam War in 1975, internal conflicts have plagued the country. From rival families and factions to colonial forces, to the single most powerful military force on the planet, the fabric of the country has been torn apart by the bloodshed of war. But the Vietnamese have come through it all, with their national identity in-tact and with a strong, unified nation.

In the late eighteenth century, two families were engaged in a bitter and bloody power struggle for control of Vietnam. The Trinh family was in open conflict with the Nguyen family who held the land in central Vietnam and the Mekong delta. To gain the upper hand, Nguyen Anh visited France to appeal for help from Versailles[1]. Little did he know, he was inviting in the country's next colonial occupiers.

With the British Empire in full flow, the government in London was reaping the spoils of their colonies and opening new trade routes for British merchants in India and the Americas. When Nguyen Anh arrived in Versailles, the French saw an opportunity in Vietnam to exploit their raw materials and economically compete with the British[2].

The French arrived to support Nguyen under the pretence of protecting the Vietnamese Catholic population. In 1859 the French captured Saigon and soon began taking over the country. The Vietnamese emperor formally conceded to French forces in 1861, and by 1893 the French occupiers were in control of Laos, Cambodia, Cochin China (modern-day southern Vietnam), Annam (modern-day central Vietnam), and Tonkin (northern Vietnam)[3].

Life Under French Rule

After centuries of Chinese repression, Vietnamese national identity was well-established. To control the population the French would need to handle the Vietnamese community with care. However, when the French arrived in the nineteenth century, they made several crucial mistakes.

Rather than take their model from the British in India, who governed the country through indigenous institutions, by preserving the national and regional culture and identity, the French embarked on a policy of assimilation[4]. They banned the existing written language based on Chinese characters and forced schools to adopt French or a new Romanised language named *quoc ngu*[5].

While the French government maintained the outward appearance of the existing Vietnamese political system, they replaced indigenous officials with French officials across all levels of government. The new French officials took over the daily running of the whole of occupied Indochina, despite very few of them having a basic grasp of the language. Even the Prime Minister, Nguyen Van Xuan, who was a French citizen, could barely speak the local Vietnamese language[6].

Economically, the colonial government did little to advance the indigenous population. The French embarked on a campaign to establish Vietnam as a leading rice exporter. They confiscated land across the country and awarded it to wealthy Catholics who supported the colonial regime. By 1945, Vietnam was the third largest rice exporter in the world, after Thailand and Burma[7]. Rather than keep the surplus rice each year as a reserve for future years with a poor harvest, the French exported as much as they could. As a result, the colonial period was riddled with famines, and the poor Vietnamese population suffered greatly.

The Vietnamese were reduced to the lower levels of government and menial labour. In 1903, the highest paid Vietnamese official still earned less than the lowest paid French government bureaucrat[8]. The French occupiers feared that allowing indigenous political institutions to form and govern, even at a regional level, would lead to the demand for more autonomy and threaten the French establishment[9]. But before long, their repression and discrimination of the local population meant their government was already under threat.

Persistent rebellions and uprisings in response to the repressive French political and economic policies flared up almost as soon as the French arrived in Vietnam. They took their toll on the European visitors and made governing the country an uphill struggle. By 1925, the British had full control over the 300 million population of India with a garrisoned force of just 5,000 British troops and officials. The French were struggling to manage the same feat with the same number of troops and a population of only 30 million[10].

In response to uprisings, the government became more repressive. They would arbitrarily detain suspects and hold them for years at a time without a trial. They would also raze entire villages and destroy the homes of any families suspected of harbouring rebels[11].

The revolts were mostly uncoordinated and occurred in pockets up and down the country. In the North, for example, Buddhists frequently attacked Vietnamese Catholics, who they accused of collaborating with the French[12]. A coherent movement almost formed under the rebel leader, Pham Dinh Phung. He established a guerrilla army in the central coastal region toward the end of the nineteenth century. However, the French authorities bribed those close to him into betraying him, and they managed to largely pacify the region by 1896 when he died from dysentery[13].

Ho Chi Minh

No examination of the birth of Vietnamese nationalism can be undertaken without mentioning Ho Chi Minh. Widely regarded as the father of Vietnam, 'Uncle' Ho was the first man to unite the sporadic rebel groups with the objective of overthrowing the French.

He was born Nguyen Sinh Cung in 1890 in central Vietnam and left the country at the age of 21 to become a galley boy on a French freighter[14]. His travels would take him first to London, then to France where he began to engage with Europe's communists, who had started to split with the socialists after the Russian revolution in 1917[15]. Throughout the early 1920s in Paris, he became obsessed with the fate of Vietnam, but his ideology and leftist belief extended little beyond activism, political debates, and demonstrations.

It wasn't until he travelled to Moscow in 1924 when his activism would transcend into political mobilisation. In Moscow, he met Stalin and Trotsky but was unimpressed by their lack of interest in Vietnam's struggle[16], so he quickly moved on to China. Ho Chi Minh began to mobilise Vietnamese students studying in Southern China and formed his first political organisation, the *Thanh Nien Cach Mang Dong Chi Hoi* or the Revolutionary Youth League[17].

The Youth League wrote political tracts and formed underground cells to rally support and interest for the plight of Vietnam under the French. In June 1929, in Hong Kong, Ho arranged a meeting between the leaders of the various communist factions in exile. With many of them being closely monitored by the British colonial police, he arranged the meeting at a football stadium during a football match to avoid detection. It was there the very first Indochinese Communist Party was formed[18]. Initially, they had one objective; to secure Vietnamese independence.

The early years of the party were eventful. Ho was arrested by the Hong Kong police for his subversive political activities and his lawyer, Frank Loseby, had to arrange his release. A British doctor diagnosed Ho with tuberculosis and arranged passage for him to England to receive treatment. After boarding the ship, the Hong Kong police deemed the move an illegal departure and rearrested him as the ship stopped in Singapore. Ho was sent to a prison infirmary. But again, he planned his escape. He recruited a hospital employee to report him dead, then escaped from the facility[19]. At the time, the global press believed the claim; his obituary even appeared in Soviet newspapers at the time.

The Second World War

In 1940, after the outbreak of war and the German invasion of France, the French forces surrendered to their German occupiers. As part of the surrender, the Japanese would take over the French colony of Indochina, as they were Germany's closest ally in the region[20].

Despite Japanese troops entering the country, Admiral Decoux of the French colonial regime remained in control of the day-to-day governing of Vietnam[21]. The Japanese were happy to let the French troops maintain law and order. From their point of view, if the French troops were occupied with preserving hold of their colony, they would not join the other allied forces waging war against Japan in the pacific.

Ho Chi Minh sensed the rumblings of opportunity on the horizon and left China to return to the country of his birth, more than 23 years after he had left. In 1941, he slipped across the Vietnamese-Chinese border disguised as a journalist[22]. He was finally home.

Ho wasted no time and formed a patriotic, nationalist organisation of Vietnamese workers, soldiers, merchants, and peasants. He named the organisation the *Viet Nam Doc Lap Dong Minh*, the Vietnam Independence League, which was eventually shortened to, Vietminh[23].

The Vietminh established a liberated zone in the north where they enjoyed the support of the people. They influenced political thought and received an endorsement from the U.S. As a fierce anti-colonialist, Franklin D. Roosevelt gave the Vietminh military equipment in return for information on the movements of Japanese troops in the country[24]. The U.S. even sent a delegation to meet Ho Chi Minh and his Vietminh in the 1940s.

In spring of 1945, the Japanese began to suspect the French colonial forces in Vietnam were planning to join the allied campaign in Asia. On March 9th, 1945, the Japanese launched a coup. The outnumbered French forces were easily defeated, and the Japanese took over the government of Vietnam[25]. Unlike their French predecessors, the Japanese instantly proclaimed Vietnam independent and allowed the Vietnamese to set-up their own legislative body and government[26] under emperor Bao Dai.

By August, the news was spreading that Japanese surrender in the Pacific was imminent. The Vietminh used this as an opportunity to strike. On the 16th of August, communists across the country attempted to seize power in what was dubbed the August Revolution[27]. In Hanoi, communists in "black pyjamas," their signature black khaki uniforms, seized the emperor's delegate. They demanded that Bao Dai resign at his palace in Hue and he succumbed to their demands. A week later, Ho Chi Minh declared Vietnam independent of the colonial or occupied rule[28].

After receiving American support under Roosevelt before the August Revolution, Ho Chi Minh was optimistic about forging a relationship with the American government. Ironically, it was during this time that he told an OSS agent he would welcome "a million American soldiers… but no French.[29]" Words that would later come back to haunt him.

When the Japanese surrendered to the allied forces on September 2nd, 1945, the Vietminh's position was no longer secure. The British, eager to keep their colonies in India, threw their support behind the French in Vietnam. They released 1,400 French troops from prison in Saigon and provided them with weapons. The following day, on September 22nd, the troops mounted an attack on Saigon[30]. They stormed public buildings, raised the French flag on rooftops, disbanded the Provisional Executive Committee in government and took control of city hall.

Having lost Saigon and the rest of Cochin China, Ho was in a difficult situation. The French had an invasion force waiting off the coast of Haiphong. The U.S. and British supported the French colonial objectives, and Ho had no allies. The USSR was uninterested in offering any support[31]. Acutely aware of his precarious situation, Ho attempted make a deal with the French. On March 6th, as French ships were approaching Haiphong harbour, Ho made a deal with the French representative, Jean Sainteny. Under the March agreement, he accepted the presence of 15,000 French troops in northern Vietnam, and in exchange, the French would acknowledge Vietnam as a free state. They would also arrange for a referendum to take place for the public to decide if they wanted the three provinces reunited[32].

The situation was precarious. The French had no intention of granting the Vietnamese a referendum. They held control of Saigon but knew that Ho still enjoyed widespread support in the south and could sway a referendum result. By the end of March, the French had still not arranged a fixed date for the referendum, and the Vietminh resumed guerrilla attacks against the colonial army in the south[33].

As the guerrilla strikes intensified and the French remained reluctant to offer any fixed referendum plans, Ho travelled to France in the summer of 1946 to discuss the March agreement. The two delegations met near Paris, in Fontainebleau. Ho offered them Vietnam back, but on the condition, the country could maintain an autonomous Vietnamese government within the French Union as a federation state linked to France[34].

David Schoenbrun, an American journalist, asked Ho what his next step would be if the French refused to grant Vietnam political autonomy. His reply was, "Why, we will fight of course.[35]"

The Outbreak of the First Indochinese War

In Fontainebleau, Ho and his delegation were unable to make any headway in their dream to unite Vietnam as an independent nation. However, after the delegation had given up and come home, Ho singlehandedly negotiated a ceasefire 'modus vivendi' in mid-September[36]. The agreement came into effect as of the 30th of October and included the installation of mixed French-Vietnamese commissions to oversee Franco-Vietnamese economic and military relations.

The guerrilla operations in the south against the French forces entirely ceased on October 30th, as agreed. The prompt cessation of hostilities demonstrates the full and extensive control Ho Chi Minh had over the movements across the country. This only further confirmed to the French that Ho's cause of a united and independent Vietnam also resonated deeply with the people of the south. To give them a referendum would see them vote for unity and effectively hand Ho Chi Minh control of the land south of the 16th parallel.

Vietnam was also essential to France's broader global position. The French knew if the Vietminh succeeded in securing independence for their small nation of Vietnam, it would send a strong message to France's African colonies who also craved independence[37]. The French were committed to retaining their Vietnamese colony at all costs.

On November 20th, a French customs patrol ship attempted to seize a Chinese vessel off the coast of the northern Vietnamese city of Haiphong. Vietnamese authorities intervened to prevent the seizure, which provided the spark the French needed to escalate the military conflict with the Vietminh further[38]. In retaliation, French forces attacked strategic positions in Haiphong and the following day shelled the city with artillery, killing thousands of Vietnamese and paving the way for French troops to secure the city.

Even in the face of this overt French aggression, Ho still hoped for a peaceful solution. He sent telegrams to the French foreign minister, Leon Blum, in Paris begging for peace[39]. Unfortunately, the telegrams didn't arrive until December 20th, the day after war broke out.

In the weeks following the French seizure of Haiphong, French officials launched a crackdown on Vietnamese dissidents. In the third week of December, French officers killed several citizens in Hanoi in the name of French "reprisals." Fearing a repeat of what occurred in Haiphong, the Tu Ve, the local Vietminh defence forces, attacked the French troops to preserve their city.

In the morning of the 20th, the Vietminh expected a full-blown French retaliation, so the order was given to attack the French that evening. However, no retaliation came, and that afternoon the order was receded. But in an environment of confusion, the French got wind of the previously planned attack and retreated their troops to the barracks in the city. Upon seeing the movement of French forces and regrouping in the barracks, the Vietminh interpreted it as an indication the French were regrouping for an attack and resumed their original attack plans. At eight o'clock, on the evening of December 20th, the Vietminh attacked the French forces in an uncoordinated and confused attack[40]. This time, the French did retaliate and took critical public buildings. When the dust had settled, Hanoi was in the hands of the colonial forces.

With that, amidst a flurry of confusion and misinterpretation, a war erupted in Indochina that would begin with the French and end with the Americans, spread across three countries in the region and span almost 30 years.

Dien Bien Phu

The Vietminh guerrilla movement wreaked havoc for the French forces across the countryside. In the years following the outbreak of war, the Vietminh enjoyed the support of the rural communities, while the French colonial forces controlled the cities[41].

It was during this period of fighting that Washington increasingly began to see the conflict in Vietnam as a communist matter, rather than nationalist. In 1947, Truman's advisors began to suggest that Ho Chi Minh's Vietminh army was more than just a nationalist force. By 1949 Secretary of State Dean Acheson was confident Ho was "as much nationalist as Commie[42]." It was here the American policy towards Vietnam began to take shape. By the end of the First Indochinese War, the U.S. had extended more than $2.6 billion of aid to the French, making up around 78% of the French war effort[43].

Since 1947, the French forces had been in conversation with the emperor in exile, Bao Dai, to lure him back to the Vietnamese throne[44]. But he had refused to return to Vietnam until the French assured him they would unify the country as one free and independent state. To pacify the situation in Vietnam, the French agreed to his terms and on March 8th, 1949, he travelled to Paris to sign the Elysée agreement. The agreement was between two leaders in the figurehead emperor Bao Dai and French figurehead President, Vincent Auriol. The French agreed to give the Vietnamese independence and unite Colchinchina with the rest of Vietnam, however, they would retain control of Vietnam's finances, military policy, and foreign policy, in a deal that only granted the illusion of independence[45]. Not only was Ho Chi Minh against the deal, he saw Bao Dai's government as illegitimate and the emperor as a French puppet[46].

But Ho Chi Minh's forces were not without their supporters. In 1949 Mao's Chinese Communist Party completed his Chinese revolution and defeated Chiang Kai-shek's forces, pushing them out of mainland China. Therefore, at the end of 1949, Mao could extend more assistance to the Vietminh war effort. He provided weapons and equipment to Ho and Giap's troops and offered them sanctuaries across the border in China from which they could launch attacks. He also offered them the opportunity to train forces with the Chinese People's Army[47]. At the time, weapons in China were plentiful as the U.S. had sent Chiang Kai-shek's forces plenty of equipment which had been lost in battle and was now in the hands of the Chinese communists.

The French search for peace hadn't worked, and with the Vietminh enjoying increased Chinese support, the war entered a new dangerous stage.

In 1953, the French established a fortress in Western Tonkin at Dien Bien Phu[48]. The intention was to use the strategic location of West Tonkin as a "mooring point" from which to launch attacks in the north, to the rear of General Vo Nguyen Giap's army[49]. But the fortress was relatively isolated and required airlifted supplies. General Giap spied the opportunity to gain the upper hand in the war and strike a heavy blow to the French forces when on the 13th of March 1954, he moved his forces in position to lay siege to the fortress. He described his objectives afterward; "We decided to wipe out at all costs the whole enemy force at Dien Bien Phu.[50]"

To achieve this objective, Giap positioned 70,000 men at the fortress and along communication lines. In comparison, the French had a force of around 13,000, only half of which were combat trained[51]. Initially, Giap unleashed a "human wave" at the French positions, on the recommendation of the Chinese, suffering heavy losses. Later in the afternoon, he changed his approach. Instead, the Vietminh encircled the French with a network of trenches and tunnels and slowly strangled the remaining French forces in a battle of guerrilla attrition over the next two weeks.

The U.S. considered offering air support to the French during the siege. The plans included B-52 bombers launching night strikes on the dug in Viet Minh positions. It was General Matthew Ridgway who persuaded Eisenhower it was the wrong war at the wrong time[52] and could lead to another direct conflict with China. The French were disappointed, but American intervention in Vietnam was delayed a while longer.

The Departure of the French

In early 1953, the Americans, Chinese and North Korean delegations agreed to a peace armistice in Korea. Simultaneously, Stalin was promoting peace in Asia, and a conference was due to take place over the fate of Germany. In this atmosphere of peace, the French were becoming eager to bring an end to the war in Indochina[53].

This terrified U.S. Secretary of State John Foster Dulles. He believed the Korean communists had only agreed to a ceasefire under pressure from the Chinese to allow them to divert their resources to Vietnam instead. He urged the French not to consider making a deal with Ho Chi Minh and gave the French forces $500 million to further convince them not to leave Vietnam to the communists.

The French had entered the Geneva conference before their loss at Dien Bien Phu, but after their military disaster and total defeat, they were even more eager to bring an end to the conflict[54]. Given the weakened position from which the French approached the Geneva conference, they could expertly manipulate Pham Van Dong and the Vietminh delegation at the negotiating table. The Vietminh agreed to establish a demarcation line along the 17th parallel. They held the territory in the north, while the French retreated to the south. Emperor Bao Dai would stand aside and appoint a new premier in the south, Ngo Dinh Diem. Diem and the French administration in the south would organise national elections in 1956 to unify the whole country[55]. Crucially, although in attendance, the U.S. refused to sign the Geneva agreement, so its contents would not bind them later[56].

After such a huge victory and Dien Bien Phu and widespread support, the Vietminh still accepted a deal which kept French troops in the south and a country divided along the 17th parallel. The only explanation as to why the Vietminh delegation accepted such unfavourable terms, is the Vietminh were cautious of the nature of the Franco-American relationship. After the end of the Korean conflict, the Vietminh were aware of Truman's domino theory and the American commitment to contain communism across the globe. They didn't want to draw out an American attack[57].

After seven years of war, an underwhelming ceasefire agreement resulted in an equally divided Vietnam. The fault lines that existed in 1946 before the war began still plagued the country. Vietnam's new premier, Ngo Dinh Diem forebodingly, yet accurately prophesized after the Geneva conference, "another more deadly war" was on its way to Vietnam.

Chapter 2 – Out of the Frying Pan, Into the Fire: The Government of Ngo Dinh Diem

The French, indifferent regarding who should be made Prime Minister, influenced the choice to appoint Ngo Dinh Diem. He wasn't a natural leader and was unknown to the Vietnamese population as he spent 1953 living in a Benedictine monastery in Belgium and socialising with the Vietnamese in exile in Paris[58]. But there were very few other options. In the wake of the first Indochinese War, there were very few capable Vietnamese leaders who were not communists or in the north[59].

The Americans threw their support behind Diem because, in the words of John Foster Dulles, "we knew of no one better.[60]" This was certainly true; there was a distinct lack of alternative candidates. But also, Diem sat well with the American establishment. At the time, the U.S. was experiencing a religious revival. They saw communism as a godless ideology and Diem, as a Christian, was a good choice to face off against the northern, godless, Vietnamese communists. There was also a belief among American politicians that Asian leaders were passive and incapable. Diem's authoritarian nature broke the mould and appealed to the American government. They were sold on their "miracle man" and more than happy to give Diem their backing[61].

Diem had so much American support behind him, which even before the Geneva conference had finished, on June 1st, 1954, CIA agent, Colonel Edward Lansdale was dispatched to Saigon with the mission of setting up a pro-American regime in the south with Diem as Prime Minister[62].

At the conference, the unwavering American support of Diem became a source of a rift in the Franco-American relationship. French diplomats warned of the potential chaos and tragedy that would occur if Diem became Prime Minister. It was under this cloud of disagreement over Diem that France decided to withdraw from Vietnam. War had broken out in Algeria, another French colony, and the French government needed all the resources it could muster. With the feeling of a government jumping from a sinking ship, the French left Vietnam to its fate with Diem at the helm of the American engineered Vietnamese vessel.

Diem's Authoritarian Regime

Diem kept his power very close. Diem and his brother, Ngo Dinh Nhu, controlled the police, the military, and the civil administration for the state of Vietnam south of the 17th parallel almost singlehandedly[63]. He relied on the U.S. to train the police and army in methods of oppression and frequently dispatched them to silence those who subverted his authority. Under Diems time in government, 12,000 suspected Vietminh were rounded up and executed, with a further 50,000 serving prison sentences. In 1959, when Diem attempted to further shore up his power base, he streamlined the process so much that anyone accused of treason could be tried and executed within three days of their initial arrest[64].

He also destroyed any semblance of village democracy. He believed the villages were infiltrated with Vietminh communists, so he removed the village councils and appointed his own village chiefs. The majority of these were selected from his supporters, many of whom were Catholics fleeing the North[65]. Diem believed he needed to control the villages to stop the spread of communist ideals and, as a result, the rural communities were hit hardest by many of his policies. He aggressively pursued a land reform program. The Army of the Republic of Vietnam (ARVN) would enter a village and forcibly take the land from the peasants, many of whom had been legally and legitimately awarded the land by the Vietminh during the war with the French. Unsatisfied at merely stripping the peasants of their land and livelihood, Diem charged them rent for the periods they had occupied the land.[66].

The Implementation of American Democracy

Almost as soon as Lansdale arrived in Vietnam, he organised a paramilitary group called Binh. They began carrying out acts of sabotage on the buses and trains north of the 17th parallel[67]. The move was a clear signal of the American contempt for the agreement hashed out in Geneva between the Vietminh and the French. The U.S. also initiated *Operation Passage to Freedom*. They dispersed propaganda north of the 17th parallel designed to undermine the Vietminh government in the north and spread fear among the Catholic population to incite them into fleeing southwards. Between 1954 and 1955, almost one million people fled the north to the south[68]. Many persuaded into it by American propaganda and the vague promise of a better life.

Lansdale quickly became Diem's guardian angel. He handled any domestic challenges to Diem's authority pragmatically and promptly. When he got wind of a planned military coup from General Nguyen Van Hinh, Lansdale promptly dispatched the general's co-conspirators and lieutenants to a meeting in the Philippines, removing them from the country and nullifying the threat. When Diem's repressive and authoritarian policies angered the Hoa Hao and Cao Dai religious sects, Lansdale paid key figures within the groups as much as $3 million to turn their support back to Diem[69]. When the ARVN finally got the opportunity, they could capture Hoa Hao leader, Ba Cut, and publicly guillotined him in 1956.

But, Diem's most significant threat by far, came in the spring of 1955. The Binh Xuyen sect, led by Bay Vien, rallied 40,000 troops and attacked government outposts in Saigon. They enjoyed the support of the French, who assisted the Binh Xuyen by sharing intelligence and obstructing Diem's troops. By the end of April, Saigon resembled a battleground. Bao Dai called Diem to France, to pacify the situation, but Diem refused. Bao Dai's generals joined the Binh Xuyen in their attempt to oust him. By the end of May, after a month of fighting, Diem's forces gained the upper hand, and the Binh Xuyen troops were routed. Bay Vien fled to France and the remaining Binh Xuyen, Cao Dai and Hoa Hao troops escaped to the Mekong delta where they would join the hiding communist cells and form the basis for what would be known as the Vietcong guerrillas in 1960[70].

After holding onto his government by the skin of his teeth, Diem was determined to ensure Bao Dai could not use his political might against him again. Diem arranged for elections to take place between him and Bao Dai in October 1955 to put an end to the old emperor's political aspirations once and for all.

The election itself had American fingerprints all over it. Lansdale designed the election ballots to appeal to the Vietnamese sense of good luck and fortune. He put Diem's name in red, a colour which signifies good fortune in Vietnam, while Bao Dai's name was printed in green, a colour of misfortune in Vietnamese culture[71]. Diem's supporters also put an enormous amount of pressure on voters to vote for their candidate. One voter described the election in a village near Hue. "They told us to put the red ballot into the envelope and throw the green ones into the wastebasket.[72]" Those who did vote for Bao Dai were reportedly followed away from the polling station and beaten up. When polls closed, Diem assumed the presidency of the Republic of Vietnam, carrying 98.2%[73] of the votes.

Diem's Commitment to Security

As the deadline for the July 1956 elections to unify the country crept ever nearer, Diem made no secret of his reluctance to allow them to go ahead. He ignored calls to set an election date because as he never signed the Geneva agreement himself, he was not bound by its contents. The French and the Vietminh negotiated the deal, neither of which were in control of the Republic of Vietnam. Therefore nothing agreed at Geneva still stood[74].

There was, of course, far more to it than that. Eisenhower later admitted he believed the Vietminh would have won 80% of the vote had the elections been allowed to take place[75]. The U.S. was, therefore, adamantly against the idea of holding free elections which would likely involve turning the country over to the communists. They weren't the only ones. The USSR suggested making the 17th parallel partition permanent and called for the international recognition of the Republic of Vietnam and the Democratic Republic of Vietnam as two separate states. This did not sit well with Eisenhower and Dulles, who had no intention of offering Ho Chi Minh's Democratic Republic of Vietnam international recognition[76].

In response to Diem's refusal to acknowledge the terms of the Geneva agreement, Ho Chi Minh wanted to restart the war with the south immediately. However, he hesitated. Ho was concerned he would not have the Sino-Soviet support he desperately needed to take on the regime in the south. Diem had the unwavering support of Washington, and he feared U.S. military intervention should he reignite a conflict to unify the country[77]. The time would come for a war when his government was established, and he had the opportunity to make the necessary preparations. For now, he had to be patient.

In the wake of the election, Diem fiercely pursued any remaining communists and political opponents hiding in the south of the country[78]. By the end of 1956, Diem had crushed 90% of the communist cells living in the Mekong delta[79]. Those who remained were forced to hide in remote areas. But his techniques did not do him any favours.

Diem viewed the rural communities as hotbeds of potential communist insurgents. His aggressive policies for handling the provinces became intensely focused neutralising potential threats and bringing security to the countryside. He introduced *agrovilles* in the late 1950s. The agroville program uprooted peasants from their native villages and communities and forced them to live in large government-run farms. The reasoning behind it was the population could be easily managed from a government controlled community.

Rather than bring the rural population onto Diem's side, his agroville policy only served to alienate his government from the rural communities further. The scheme was poorly thought out and poorly executed. Uprooting peasants from their ancestral lands caused distress and resentment from the communities. Corruption meant the promised supplies didn't always get to the agrovilles and there were often more people crammed in than the farms could employ. In one case an agroville with enough land to employ 6,000 peasants on the farms, had 14,000 Vietnamese farmers working[80] in it. The extra workers were essentially working without pay in conditions little better than forced labour.

His obsession on controlling the provinces, rather than nurturing them, meant that despite receiving more than $1 billion in aid from his American backers, he spent little on education, healthcare, and other public services[81]. Medical bills were beyond most family's financial capabilities, and many children in the provinces could not attend school due to poor infrastructure. Rather than appoint competent statesmen and officials to run the provinces, he preferred to appoint military officials in provincial government positions. By 1962, 36 out of the 40 province chiefs were military officials[82]. Most were Catholics Diem could trust and rarely interacted with the communities they were supposed to represent. By viewing the provincial regions as a problem which needed controlling rather than building-up and supporting, he was turning many against him and rallying support for the communist cause.

This was reflected in the number of guerrilla attacks and assassinations. In 1957, after Diem's crackdown in the Mekong delta, the communist cells in the south assassinated 400 government officials[83]. This figure swelled to 1,200 in 1959 and 4,000 a year by 1961[84].

One bus driver recounts his memories of this time. A small group of guerrillas stopped his bus and came on board. They approached two men sitting on the bus and calmly checked their identity cards. The leader of the group told the two men they had been warned many times to stop cooperating with the government, yet they had still not quit their jobs. The guerrilla fighters removed the two men from the bus and beheaded them with machetes right there at the roadside. It turned out the two men were policemen working for the government[85].

Act Now or Risk Losing the South Forever

In 1959, Le Duan, a veteran communist who had helped manage Ho Chi Minh's war effort against the French in the south, managed to persuade Ho Chi Minh that unless he acted soon, he would lose the south of Vietnam forever[86]. This ignited a flurry of covert activity along the 17th parallel and in the guerrilla cells in the south.

Ho immediately reopened the Ho Chi Minh Trail, the intricate network of roads and jungle trails which ran the length of the country. He began transporting administrators loyal to him, but native southerners to help organise the guerrilla cells in the south. It was in 1960 these elusive communist cells untied and formed their own state in the south in competition with Diem's government. They called themselves the National Liberation Front (NLF) and their army, the People's Liberation Armed Forces (PLA)[87]. Their objectives were to overthrow Diem's government and open negotiations with Hanoi to unify the country[88]. Although they relied on the support of the Vietminh, they were different from their northern counterparts, and in the years after the war, the NLF would clash with the northern communist government on the running of the country.

The southern communists organised their military into 37 companies based out of the Mekong delta. It was essential to Ho the companies received their troops and supplies from the north in absolute secrecy. It was essential to Ho he at least maintained the outward appearance of adhering to the Geneva agreement[89].

While Ho was conjuring illusions in the North, Diem was in the south. To continue the steady stream of American aid, Diem needed to pretend at least his government was democratic. In 1959, he organised legislative elections to keep up the democratic illusion. Unlike the previous election against Bo Dai, voters were registered, and the ballots were kept secret. Diem also permitted his critics to run and campaign against his candidates in meaningful opposition. However, on the election day, it became apparent the election was anything but democratic and fair. Diem's officials stuffed ballot boxes, opposing candidates were unexpectedly disqualified for obscure financial and legal irregularities, and Diem's supporters were transported to different provinces to cast their votes where they were needed[90]. The whole election was a sham to maintain American support.

Diem would say or do anything he needed to hold onto power. Holding fraudulent elections, uprooting peasants and forcing them into slave labour, and offering the country empty reform promises. In November 1960 disgruntled soldiers from three paratrooper battalions and a unit of ARVN marines laid siege to Diem's palace in Saigon. They demanded he implements reforms. Diem fled into his palace basement and released a speech agreeing to free elections and liberal reforms. As he spoke, soldiers still loyal to him arrived in Saigon and wiped out the besieging force, leaving over 400 bodies of soldiers and citizens littering the Saigon streets[91].

Chapter 3 – Pragmatism and Idealism

In 1960, John F. Kennedy narrowly defeated Richard Nixon with 303 electoral votes to 219, ushering in a new era for American involvement in Vietnam. The Kennedy administration began escalating the extent of U.S. involvement in Vietnam that continued over the next eight years. Before Kennedy's inauguration, the U.S. had a presence of 900 advisors in Vietnam. By the time of his assassination, the U.S. had 16,000 advisors involved in combat missions with the ARVN and were providing significant aerial support[92].

Despite the apparent escalation, historians and commentators have long disagreed over what American involvement in Vietnam would have looked like had John F. Kennedy lived.

Ahead of his inauguration in 1961, Kennedy had been a supporter of providing funding to the French war effort against the Vietnamese communists and a strong backer of Ngo Dinh Diem's regime. He had also publicly called Vietnam, "a proving ground for democracy in Asia" and a "test of American responsibility and determination.[93]" Although this would indicate Kennedy's position towards Vietnam was dictated by his ideological stance, at times he handled Vietnam pragmatically, with minute care and precision and relied far more on the opinions of experts than on his own ideological belief.

Kennedy's Escalation

President Kennedy received a baptism of fire upon entering the Oval Office. Richard Nixon's bitter criticism of Kennedy on the campaign trail had hinged on him being "soft" on communism. The criticism must have stung, because in his first few months in office, in an attempt to silence his critics, he conducted an invasion of Cuba at the Bay of Pigs.

The invasion was botched and failed. He then confronted the USSR over the partition of Germany and was belittled and manipulated by Khrushchev in Vienna. By the end of his first year in office, rather than silence his critics, he had only reinforced what they suspected. Kennedy knew he needed to use Vietnam as his theatre to show the American public he could be tough on communism.

In 1961 Kennedy dispatched a task force to Southern Vietnam. George Ball would lead the project, designed to initiate military, economic and political programs with the explicit objective of preventing the communist absorption of Southern Vietnam[94]. To ensure the success of these objectives he sent 100 military advisors to support Diem's regime. In keeping with the Geneva agreement, he was careful to disperse the advisors around the country as a military build-up was in violation of the Geneva Accords.

Ngo Dinh Diem needed American support but was reluctant to allow American troops into Vietnam. In the summer of 1961, he sent Kennedy a letter asking for more assistance. Diem wanted to expand the ARVN to 270,000 troops. He wanted an aid package to help him achieve this figure, which would include more U.S. military advisors, military equipment, and weapons, along with significant financial aid[95]. Unsure of how to respond, Kennedy delayed the decision. He decided to send his trusted military advisor, General Maxwell Taylor on a visit to Vietnam in October to assess the situation and report back with his recommendations.

The ARVN's battle with the guerrilla forces intensified through the summer and into the Autumn, Diem was becoming desperate. He adjusted his demands to include a "symbolic" presence of American troops and a bilateral defence pact with his American allies.

Kennedy continued to put off the decision until after Taylor's fact-finding mission. At the end of 1961, Taylor was ready to make his recommendation after a two-week tour of the Republic of Vietnam. His recommendations presented to Kennedy involved the commitment of three squadrons of helicopters and an increase in the number of military advisors present in the country[96]. Off the record, Taylor privately suggested to Kennedy he deploys 8,000 combat troops to the Mekong delta under the guise of providing flood relief to the region. Kennedy asked Taylor what he thought about the possibility of a northern retaliation from Ho Chi Minh's government. Taylor dismissed the idea. He believed even if there were any retaliatory action, a pre-emptive bombing spree in the north would prevent them from embarking on an invasion of the south.

There were voices from others who had been on the State Department tour in 1961 who cautioned against involvement. Sterling Cottrell, a State Department specialist who accompanied Maxwell, believed a war in Vietnam would be one that "foreign military forces themselves cannot win.[97]" He recognised that Diem's support was already wavering and the war would be fought in the villages and rural communities. He concluded it would simply be unwinnable.

But in Washington, there were plenty of hawks. Secretary of Defence, Robert McNamara believed 8,000 boots on the ground wouldn't be anywhere near enough to secure military dominance. He called for a support force of 200,000 troops to be deployed in Southern Vietnam[98]. Kennedy asked Dean Rusk and McNamara to draw up a package which didn't involve combat troops. The final package Kennedy approved committed more military advisors and the recommended helicopter squadrons but stopped short of sending combat troops to Vietnam.

The military advisers, on the recommendation of Robert Thompson, a British counterinsurgency specialist, modernised Diem's agroville program and changed the objectives slightly. The new format was to create strategic hamlets where the peasants would live together and defend themselves against the NLF guerrillas. The program was designed to create a genuine resistance movement in the provinces against the spread of communism.

Much like the agroville program, the strategic hamlet program was a failure. The peasants who relocated were forced to erect fences and construct defensive positions around the fortresses to protect themselves from the enemy. But the enemy had no intention of harming peasants, only government officials. The rural communities quickly began to question the value of working to protect themselves from an enemy who had no desire to hurt them, all for the sake of the government.

The execution of the program was bungled from start to finish. Corruption meant the promised supplies often didn't reach the peasants. There were also several cases of NLF guerrillas being placed inside the strategic hamlets. From there they could influence the population and turn information over to their communist comrades on the outside[99].

Nothing demonstrates the extent to which strategic hamlets further enabled the communists than the program's leadership. The chief Lieutenant for the scheme was Colonel Pham Ngoc Thao. He rolled out strategic hamlets nationally a breakneck pace. In a matter of weeks, the fortresses littered the countryside across the Republic of Vietnam. It later emerged that Thao was a secret communist sympathizer operating from within Diem's government[100]. He promoted the program with such enthusiasm because he wanted to exploit the weak policy to aid the communist cause further. His continued eagerness for the scheme only serves to demonstrate the extent that the hamlets alienated Diem from the rural population and drove the communities into the hands of the communists.

Kennedy the Pragmatist vs. Kennedy the Idealist

It is easy to look at Kennedy's public discourse and the numbers of military advisors he committed to the assistance of Diem's government and conclude that his ideological convictions led him to put the U.S. on the path of escalation. But the bulk of this commitment came after his challenging first year in government when he needed to save face and appear strong on communism.

In contrast, Kennedy withdrew 1,000 military advisors shortly before his death in 1963[101]. Kenneth O'Donnell Jr., the son of one of Kennedy's senior advisors, Kenneth O'Donnell, remembers a conversation his father had with him in 1963. He explicitly told his son Kennedy wanted to withdraw the advisors after the election and get U.S. personnel out of Vietnam.

If Kennedy had wanted to commit more troops to Vietnam, he certainly had the opportunity. Taylor recommended committing combat troops and McNamara's call for 200,000 American troops in Vietnam would have been appealing to him.

But despite Kennedy's idealist discourse, behind the scenes, his policy towards Vietnam shows an expert balance of pragmatism and idealism[102]. When Diem asked for aid to fight the communist insurgency, he didn't automatically grant it, but sent advisors on a fact-finding mission and seriously considered the impact his decision would have on the country.

He walked a fine line to manage the electorate and appease the hawks in his government, but understood the challenge of Vietnam required, as he told a group of visiting members from Latin American Air Forces, "sophisticated techniques to meet it." In the period preceding his assassination, his sophisticated techniques would be put under intense scrutiny and tested to their very limits.

Chapter 4 – The Death of Two Catholic Presidents

Meanwhile, in the north, Ho Chi Minh's government's priority was avoiding taking action that would give the United States an excuse to commit combat troops to Vietnam. During a conversation between Pham Van Dong, Prime Minister of the Democratic Republic of Vietnam, and Bernard Fall, a French scholar, in 1962, Pham Van Dong expressed his delight with the war the guerrilla movement was waging in the south. He believed, somewhat optimistically, the U.S. would withdraw their military advisers from the country before long out of battle weariness and exhaustion[103].

Although the belief may have been a little premature, the NLF was displaying impressive battlefield tactics. Kennedy's helicopter squadrons were experiencing dwindling results after their initial success. The NLF cells had adapted quickly. Group 559 was the name given the northern Vietnamese unit tasked with transferring supplies along the Ho Chi Minh trail to the NLF cells in Southern Vietnam. They quickly transported mortars to the Southern Vietnamese guerillas to use in their effort against the U.S. helicopters[104]. They also dug trenches and tunnels to conceal their movements[105] and nullify the effectiveness of the aerial attacks.

The Battle of Ap Bac

In January 1963, the NLF scored a significant victory against Diem's ARVN. The U.S. got information that three NLF companies were positioned at Ap Bac, to the south of Saigon. They decided to formulate a plan of attack to neutralise their targets. January 2nd was the date chosen, so the U.S. helicopter pilots could fully recover from their New Year's Eve festivities before the attack. But the guerrillas caught wind of the impending allied attack and dug in defensively in preparation[106].

Despite being outnumbered 10 to 1[107], the guerrillas stood their ground and waited for the incoming ARVN troops. The diary of the Vietcong commander was later found after the attack. Within it he had written, "better to fight and die than run and be slaughtered[108]."

The ARVN Seventh division, with U.S. aerial support, began their attack on the morning of the 2nd by dropping an infantry regiment to the north of the Vietcong positions. The guerrillas opened fire on the helicopters and incoming troops with so much success that by noon five American helicopters had been downed. The rifle squadron located to the west of Ap Bac was deployed in their armoured vehicles to rescue the downed helicopter crews, but entered the melee individually and were easily picked off by the Vietcong forces. The bulk of the ARVN forces were due to attack on foot from the south. However, Major Tho, the officer in charge of the two battalions approaching from the south, stopped their advance after losing an officer. He would not be persuaded to resume the attack[109].

Feeling the battle slipping through their fingers, the ARVN deployed paratroopers to the west of the battlefield to turn the tide. But by this point, the light was fading, and they had difficulty differentiating between friend and foe. In the act of almost absurd calamity, the paratroopers fired on ARVN troops, mistaking them for Vietcong guerrillas[110]. The Vietcong companies disappeared and escaped under cover of darkness.

The following morning the U.S. and ARVN took stock of the situation. They found three Vietcong bodies among the dead. A demoralizing discovery after losing 61 ARVN troops and suffering 100 casualties[111].

The victory for the Vietcong went much further than the number of casualties inflicted. The poorly equipped NLF soldiers had taken on armoured vehicles and American helicopters and won. These had been the ARVN and U.S. trump cards, but they still hadn't been able to ensure their victory. The mental victory was far more critical to the guerrillas, the fear of American aerial support and armoured vehicles were gone, with forces across the country taking inspiration from their comrades at Ap Bac[112].

There was no time for Diem to lick his wounds. His popularity was still in sharp decline, and in February, an assassination attempt was made on his life. Two fighter aircraft from his government air force flew over his palace, dropping napalm and bombs, and spraying the building with machine gun fire[113]. Thirty officials were injured and three killed but unfortunately for the attackers, neither Diem nor his family was among the bodies. They had escaped to the reinforced palace basement after the first bomb fell.

In the wake of the assassination attempt, Diem further shored up his power base by concentrating the power within his family even more. His brother extended his spy network in the army to ensure only those loyal to the Diem regime received a promotion. But the regime's popularity was plummeting. The army believed they had no interest in defeating the Vietcong guerrillas. The troops believed they only wanted to keep the war going to maintain a constant flow of U.S. aid. The people thought the Diem family were corrupt and just governing to line their own pockets. Both statements were probably correct, but the Diem brothers didn't seem phased. When a reporter told Nhu, Diem's brother, the public believed he was corrupt and dishonest, he responded with, "I don't care what the people think."[114]

The people had every right to be angry. In the seven years since Diem came to power, nothing had changed. The U.S. had funnelled $1 billion[115] into the country, yet Diem had not conquered the Vietcong insurgency, he had also failed to win over the rural communities and, if anything, had done nothing to improve his popularity since he came to power.

A Buddhist "Barbecue"

Just when Diem's government couldn't get any worse, it was to reach new depths as their repressive measures became more concentrated against the Buddhist population.

In early May, Buddhists across Vietnam gathered to celebrate the Buddha's birthday publicly. A Catholic official in Hue decreed that Buddhists would not be allowed to carry the multicoloured flag often associated with the celebrations. To add insult to the local Buddhist population, the authorities cancelled a radio address by the influential Buddhist leader, Tri Quang. A crowd gathered outside the radio station to protest the repressive and unfair measures. When the crowd refused to disperse and end the peaceful protest, government soldiers opened fire on them, killing eight children and one woman[116] in the chaos.

Buddhist cells of dissidence spread across the country. Unlike the disenchanted peasants in rural communities, the Buddhist movement was highly educated and spoke excellent English. They briefed foreign journalists and almost immediately Diem's repressive measures, and slaughter of innocent civilians was all over the international media. They pleaded Diem to make liberal reforms and begged the American government to replace him as Prime Minister.

Confronted by an international outcry and probing American questions, Diem denied all government involvement and responsibility. He blamed the deaths in Hue on the Vietcong guerrillas shooting and creating a stampede across the crowd. To appease his

American backers, he also set up a committee to investigate the Buddhist grievances[117].

But nothing struck a chord with the international community more than the scenes at a busy Saigon intersection on the 11th of June 1963. In the morning commuter traffic, an elderly monk got out of a car and calmly approached the middle of the busy crossroads. He sat down amid the dense flurry of Saigon traffic. His fellow monks encircled him and began to douse him in petrol, drawing looks of astonishment form the pedestrians and passing vehicles. Without warning, as the man sat praying, they set him alight. As the yellow flames danced across his orange robe and licked his face, Malcolm Browne took his photo, in what would become one of the most iconic photographs in the history of photojournalism. The Buddhist community had forewarned Browne of the planned self-immolation and invited him to document the occasion. As the monk burnt, his colleagues handed out reports to the press and bystanders gathered in amazement. The reports detailed the reasons for the defiant act of public suicide. The monk, named Thich Quang Duc, called on Diem to respect the Buddhist religion and show "clarity and compassion[118]."

If anyone was in doubt over Diem and his family's concern for the incident, his sister-in-law, Madame Nhu, told a journalist, "let them burn, and we shall clap her hands," calling the spectacle a Buddhist "barbecue[119]." To add further insult to the plight of the Vietnamese Buddhists, Diem's Buddhist committee released their findings shortly after the incident. The committee maintained the Vietcong, not the government forces, had been the cause of the deaths in Hue.

Throughout the summer of 1963, some Buddhist monks burnt themselves to death in protest of Diem's government. But Diem's response was only to meet their protest with more repression. On August 21st, troops loyal to Diem's brother launched coordinated attacks against Buddhist pagodas across Saigon and other major southern cities. They arrested more than 400 nuns and monks in

Saigon. This was to become a tipping point, both for Diem's cabinet and his U.S. supporters.

In protest at the blatant disregard for the Buddhist population, Diem's Foreign Minister shaved his head in solidarity with the repressed Buddhists. It was when Diem's cabinet turned against him that the U.S. finally decided it was time to replace the heavy-handed Catholic Prime Minister.

The End of Ngo Dinh Diem

Kennedy's administration was divided over the issue. Dean Rusk and George Ball initially gave their consent to a coup to overthrow Diem. Their opponents were Vice President, Lyndon Johnson, Secretary of State, Robert McNamara, and General Maxwell Taylor. The Diem issue represented the first major split in the Kennedy administration.

After four days of intense arguing, Henry Cabot Lodge, the American Ambassador to Saigon, weighed in on the situation. He pushed for Kennedy to give the army rebels the green light to overthrow Diem. Secret microphones recording the deliberations show John F. Kennedy's concern. "We're up to our hips in mud out there," he mused. He knew Congress would be annoyed at the overthrow of Diem but concluded "they'll be madder if Vietnam goes down the drain.[120]"

In the end, Kennedy gave the green light. On the 1st of November, troops surrounded Diem's palace and took control of the radio stations. Diem and his brother fled the palace that evening to the house of the wealthy Chinese merchant, Ma Tuyen, a financier of their regime in the town of Cholon.

After Diem issued his unconditional surrender, soldiers were dispatched from Saigon to collect him and his brother, but they never made it back to the city. General Xuan, the general in charge of the operation, had his men assassinate the pair at a railroad crossing[121].

When Kennedy heard of Diem's death, he expressed intense shock and abhorrence at the situation[122]. But he had been naïve to expect the Vietnamese generals would permit Diem and his brother to live. They couldn't exile him to the U.S. as his presence there would have embarrassed the Kennedy administration for their previous support of his repressive and unpopular regime. He couldn't stay in Vietnam under a new leader and finding another location for him to live in exile required diplomatic negotiation.

His death was greeted with alarm in Hanoi. Ho Chi Minh's government believed this committed the U.S. to Southern Vietnam and increased the chances of their military involvement. They immediately dispatched more assistance to the south, hoping in the event of an imminent war they could take Saigon before the U.S. could intervene[123].

Less than three weeks later, John F. Kennedy was assassinated in Dallas as he rode in an open top vehicle. November 1963 marks a watershed for American policy in Vietnam. The two Catholic presidents met their ends at the end of two guns and with those two isolated shots, the U.S. was committed to a war that would kill 58,000 Americans, 1.5 million Vietnamese and tear at the very fabric of American society.

Chapter 5 – Smoke and Mirrors: Johnson's War

When Lyndon Baines Johnson succeeded John F. Kennedy following his assassination, he was under no illusions about the severity of the situation in Vietnam. He had seen how Kennedy's critics had publicly crucified him for being soft in the face of expanding global communism and was determined not to let the same thing happen to him.

If people were unsure of Kennedy's real motives in Vietnam, Johnson left no such ambiguity. With the South Vietnamese Army still suffering heavy defeats at the hands of the communist guerrillas, and with Diem gone, the position of the South Vietnamese government looked precarious. Duong Van Minh succeeded Diem as Chief of State, but he lacked the strength of character to lead a country as fragmented as Vietnam and was soon replaced by General Nguyen Khanh. Johnson and his advisors decided that without U.S. military expansion, the south could not be saved. Before he could commit ground troops and expand the war, Johnson needed approval from Congress. With a bit of cunning and illusion, all the authorisation he required would shortly fall into his lap.

The Gulf of Tonkin Incident

Recently declassified documents have revealed the extent to which senior members of Johnson's administration lied and exaggerated to further commit the U.S. military to Vietnam.

In early 1964, the Southern Vietnamese navy with U.S. naval support initiated a string of covert operations off the northern Vietnamese coast. Named OPLAN 34A, they had limited success. The Southern Vietnamese ships suffered heavy casualties, and many were captured[124]. With the Southern Vietnamese navy struggling to make headway, commander of the U.S. Military Assistance Command, William Westmoreland, decided to intensify the operations. They would now include shore attacks on northern Vietnamese positions with mortars and rockets. The U.S. Navy would also begin reconnaissance missions north of the 17th parallel.

It was on one of these missions, on August 1st, 1963, that the *Maddox*, a U.S. destroyer, intercepted signals indicating that communist torpedo vessels were preparing to attack their position. It was likely retaliation for the attack on Hon Me island by the Republic of Vietnam Navy the previous night, although Captain John J. Herrick was unaware of this attack at this time[125].

When three communist vessels began to approach, Herrick ordered his men to fire on the ships once they were within 10,000 yards. The Maddox fired three warning shots across the bow of the first boat at around that distance. The torpedo vessel responded by firing a torpedo at the U.S. destroyer. The Maddox began to engage the three ships with gunfire. The skirmish left the Maddox with only minor damages. The three Vietnamese vessels sustained severe damage, with one left stranded in the sea burning[126].

Several days later, on the 4th of August, the Maddox once again reported communist vessels approaching. They described the ships approaching from all directions, despite being out at sea and nowhere near the northern Vietnamese coastline. The pilot, Commander Stockdale, was immediately dispatched from the *Ticonderoga* to assist. But when he arrived, he saw no signs of any Vietnamese vessels. "I had the best seat in the house to watch that event," he would later say, "and our destroyers were just shooting at phantom targets.¹²⁷" He reported his findings to Washington, confusing the Pentagon. Secretary of Defence McNamara asked if it was possible there had been no attack. Pacific Fleet Commander-in-Chief Admiral U.S. Grant Sharp agreed that it was a possibility.

What followed was one of the most deceptive and calculated actions to come out of a Presidential administration. It was reported a signal had been intercepted from a north Vietnamese vessel describing damage it had suffered from engaging a U.S. naval target. This was all the proof McNamara needed, and he immediately ordered Stockdale to organise a retaliatory aerial attack[128]. Stockdale was confused. He would later say, "We were about to launch a war under false pretenses, in the face of the on-scene military commander's advice to the contrary.[129]"

Stockdale was right, but what he didn't realise was this was precisely what Johnson and McNamara wanted. Later declassified information would show the intercepted signal report had been referring to the previous attack on the Maddox from several days previously, but it had been deliberately placed amongst the evidence for the August 4th attacks.

Despite his misgivings, Stockdale led an attack on an oil storage facility in northern Vietnam with 18 aircraft. In the wake of the attacks on the Maddox, Congress passed the emergency Gulf of Tonkin resolution which Johnson signed into law on the 7th of August. The resolution authorised Johnson to "take all necessary measures to repel any armed attack against the forces of the United States.[130]" The President could barely contain his delight. He had received a blank cheque from Congress to escalate the war..

Johnson showed restraint in the wake of the Gulf of Tonkin Resolution. He limited the bombing of the north to just one day after the incident. Now he had all the authority he needed; there was no need to rush anything[131]. After all, there was a presidential election coming up, and the last thing he wanted to do was make Vietnam a divisive issue.

For the communists in Northern Vietnam, the Gulf of Tonkin incident only strengthened their commitment to war. In October 1964, Hanoi sent the first complete combat regiment into Southern Vietnam. The 95th regiment included senior North Vietnamese officers, Le Trong Tan, Tran Do and Colonel Hoang Cam[132].

The incident also strengthened Chinese and Soviet support for the Northern Vietnamese cause. As it became clearer the only solution for the Vietnamese situation would be a military one, the Soviet Union began to offer the Northern Vietnamese air assistance[133]. This would be a turning point for Soviet-Northern Vietnamese relations.

Bomb them 'Back to the Stone age'

Johnson had his eye on the Vietnam prize. With the November election coming he knew he needed to walk a tightrope. He had learned from Kennedy's mistakes. He had to demonstrate enough strength to stop his opponent, Barry Goldwater, from accusing him of being soft on communism, but he had to show enough restraint to avoid being accused of taking the U.S. down the road of a full-scale war in Vietnam. His sporadic bombing raids had achieved just that, and on November 3rd, Johnson sailed to victory by 16 million votes, the most significant victory ever won by a presidential candidate[134].

Just two days before the election, on November 1st, the Vietcong had launched a stealth attack on the American air base at Bienhoa[135]. The Vietcong mortars destroyed six B-57 bombers and damaged 20 other aircraft stationed at the base[136]. The Joint Chiefs of Staff immediately called for a retaliatory bombing campaign on Vietnamese oil refineries and ammunition depots in the North, but Johnson refused. With the election two days away, he didn't want the last thing the American public saw heading into the poll booth to be American pilots bombing Vietnam. He also was worried about provoking a significant backlash from the Northern Vietnamese forces. He only had 23,000 military advisors in the country, and they would be overrun if the Northern Vietnamese government sent troops across the 17th parallel in sizeable numbers[137]. Johnson wanted to use bombing as a negotiating tool to encourage the Northern Vietnamese government to put an end to the Vietcong insurgency in the south, without drawing a Northern Vietnamese invasion[138].

A cable sent from Lyndon Johnson to Maxwell Taylor over the Christmas period provides a glimpse into where Johnson's thoughts were in the wake of his election victory. "I have never felt that this war will be won from the air, and it seems to me that what is much more needed and would be more effective is a larger and stronger use of rangers and special forces and marines[139]."

Before Johnson could further contemplate putting American boots on the ground, the Vietcong launched another damaging attack. On the 7th of February 1965, the Vietcong guerrillas attacked the U.S. airbase at Pleiku. Johnson ordered another bombing raid into the North for the following day, in keeping with his eye-for-an-eye bombing strategy[140]. But this time, McGeorge Bundy wanted to go one further. He outlined a plan for a sustained bombing campaign that would gradually increase in intensity until the North Vietnamese government would have no choice but to enter negotiations with the U.S. to end the fiery rain ripping across the country. The initial plans contained 94 targets to be hit across an 11-week period.

On the 10th of February, the Vietcong attacked the American billet at Qui Nhon. Again, Johnson issued a retaliatory bombing raid the following day. The timing of the Vietcong attack sweetened Bundy's proposal, and with the election out of the way, two days later Johnson accepted Bundy's proposed bombing campaign. The operation was known as, Rolling Thunder.

Johnson had strict limitations about where could and could not be bombed. He refused to allow targets within 30 miles of Hanoi and 10 miles from Haiphong, the heart of Northern Vietnamese industry[141]. The operation began in earnest on the 2nd of March. 104 American aircraft bombed an ammunition depot north of the dematerialized zone. Two weeks later, on the 15th, another depot was targeted. The bombing was sporadic. Every target had to be approved by U.S. Grant Sharp, then by military experts in the Pentagon for an analysis of the military significance. Once the military had given its blessing, the State Department checked the proposed target to ensure its destruction would not trigger a Northern invasion. Only once it had received approval from each organisation could the bombing raid then be carried out[142].

In May, Johnson gave the North an opportunity to bring an end to the operation. He halted the bombing raids for five days and offered the North a $1 billion post-war development package to repair their damaged infrastructure on the condition they entered ceasefire negotiations. The Northern Vietnamese government adamantly refused to cooperate, and bombing resumed on the 18th of May.

The North Vietnamese resilience to American bombing in the Spring of 1965 would prove an ominous microcosm for American failings throughout the whole conflict in Vietnam. The Vietnamese had a rural population spread out across a vast area, much of which was covered by dense jungle foliage.

Throughout 1964 and 1965, Johnson's administration relied on several false assumptions. They believed they could disrupt the constant stream of supplies to the Vietcong by bombing the Ho Chi Minh trail around the 17th parallel. But the Ho Chi Minh trail was an elaborate labyrinth of jungle paths and tunnels. It was impossible to see from the air, and the supplies could be redirected to an alternate route at any moment. The primitive bridges were something of an advantage. If an American bomb destroyed a bridge, it could be rebuilt in a matter of days, severely reducing the effectiveness of the U.S. bombing raids[143]. Also, in April 1965, General Giap signed an agreement with Luo Ruiqing and Yang Chengwu from the Chinese government. China would begin sending some of their best engineering units to help with the reconstruction of the Northern railways, roads, and bridges[144].

The U.S. also assumed the Vietnamese would be lost without ammunition depots and power plants. But by the end of 1965, 77% of ammunition depots and 60% of power plants in Northern Vietnam had been destroyed, yet they continued to fight on. The ammunition for Chinese and Soviet-made weapons could be imported from their international communist allies.

American advisors and government officials also assumed somewhere in the jungles of Vietnam there was a communist headquarters from which they ran the war effort. They imagined if they could destroy this headquarters, they could break the Vietnamese resolve and gain the upper hand. But the headquarters did not exist as they believed. It was not a physical thing but a constantly mobile group of individuals, who conducted meetings in tunnels deep within the Vietnamese jungle. The whole camp could be decamped and moved on at any time and was mostly immune to American bombing[145].

Finally, Johnson assumed that by offering money, he could buy the North Vietnamese to the negotiating table. Curtis Lemay's promise of bombing them "back to the stone age" was always going to be difficult, but the whole Rolling Thunder campaign highlighted the lack of understanding those in Washington had about the Vietnamese population, their military strategy, and their cultural values.

Boots on the Ground

As the American aerial assault got underway according to the proposals of the Joint Chiefs of Staff, General Westmoreland had a proposition of his own for President Johnson.

According to Westmoreland's estimates, some 6,000 Vietcong guerrillas were active near the coastal city of Danang. He advised the president to dispatch ground troops to protect the nearby American air base. His proposals were endorsed by the Joint Chiefs of Staff, and Johnson gave his blessing for the deployment of 3,500 marines to Danang[146].

Their arrival was less than subtle. The Marines arrived in full battle attire and rushed up the beach, precisely as their forefathers had done in Normandy and Korea. But it wasn't enemy weapons waiting for them on the beach. Only several Vietnamese women holding a banner which read, "welcome to the Gallant Marines.

While the scene probably looked almost laughable, Nguyen Ting, a Vietcong guerrilla who watched the spectacle understood the significance. "When I saw the Americans arrive, I knew the war was about to get harder- it was going to be more ferocious, and it was going to last longer.[147]"

Chapter 6 – The American War Machine

Throughout the spring of 1965, American soldiers began engaging Vietcong and North Vietnamese troops in isolated skirmishes. In response to the deployment of American troops in the South, Ho and his government in the North deployed four regiments of the People's Army of Vietnam (PAVN) down the Ho Chi Minh trail to Southern Vietnam[148].

On May 11th, the Vietcong and their Northern allies launched their largest attack of the war so far. They attacked the town of Songbe, 50 miles north of Saigon, taking the town and raiding the U.S. special forces camp on the outskirts of nearby Dong Xoai. William Westmoreland was livid. He immediately called for the deployment of 180,000 men to protect American interests in the South and for the intensification of bombing in the North[149].

In July, Johnson conceded. On the 28th of July, he increased the number of active combat troops in Vietnam to 125,000, introducing a draft call of 35,000 American civilians[150]. He also gave the order to intensify the bombing campaign. Bombings increased from 1-2 targets a week, to 10-12 per week. Over 900 flights were conducted over Vietnam each week by the middle of 1965[151]. The military continued to call for the expansion of targets to include land and rail connections to China to disrupt the constant flow of Chinese weapons and ammunition, but Johnson wouldn't allow it out of fear of prompting Chinese troops to enter the war, as they had done in Korea.

As the war escalated, Americans began using defoliants such as Agent Orange, appropriately named after the orange stripe painted across the barrels it was stored in. The American strategy involved bombing an area suspected of harbouring Vietcong guerrillas and driving the villagers out of the hamlets, often destroying all the jungle foliage with herbicidal sprays. The military would enter and kill any remaining Vietcong guerrillas left out in the open with nowhere to hide.

During 1965, the heavy bombing campaigns drove some four million refugees out of their rural villages to cities. The Americans embraced it. They believed the forced urbanisation of the rural population would stop the spread of communist support in the rural areas[152]. The strategy was highly flawed. Within a month of "clearing" a village of Vietcong elements, they would be back. Only the refugees remained displaced, eking out a living in the overpopulated towns and cities of Southern Vietnam. Every village the Americans ruined in this way, became a village of resistance and stirred up more communist sympathy.

The bombing strategies may not have been a success, but the logistical feat the Americans pulled off in Vietnam was nothing short of miraculous. The American military built roads and bridges to transport their troops and supplies. They dredged rivers to create more secure island bases; they built refrigerated warehouses, new harbours, piers, and a new communication grid across the country.

By 1967, 100lbs of equipment was pouring into the country, per soldier, per day[153]. The soldiers in Vietnam had access to American cigarette brands, their favourite beer, a separate Thanksgiving and Christmas food menu complete with turkey, a postal service, shampoo, deodorant, and plenty of condoms. A soldier based in Saigon could even buy a car and arrange to have it delivered to his house in the U.S. for when he returned home[154].

Morale was high in 1965. Americans arrived in Vietnam with confidence they would easily win the war and be home by Christmas. But that was all to change after their first serious encounter with the enemy.

Ia Drang

No single event gave the American forces as much of a reality check as the fighting in Ia Drang valley at the end of 1965. On November 14th, army intelligence indicated a strong presence of around 2,200 soldiers near Ia Drang valley[155]. The 7th Cavalry Division was deployed to root them out and eliminate them. In reality, the figure was almost three times this amount. Most of the communist forces were from the Northern People's Army and had just completed a two-month journey down the Ho Chi Minh trail from the North. Their objective from General Giap was to engage the American soldiers to see what their battle tactics were and how they would use their helicopters.

The 450 troops dispatched to Ia Drang came under fire. One B company platoon was almost instantly cut off from their support. By the time the platoon was rescued three days later when the fighting had died down, some 20 of the 27 soldiers had been killed or wounded[156]. The 450 troops were pinned down for the whole of the first day. It was only thanks to a helicopter dropping off an additional U.S. battalion that prevented the total collapse and elimination of the American forces. Lt. Harold G. Moore would later describe the attack. He described how the Northern Vietnamese troops were masters of camouflage and fought with dogged determination, sometimes continuing to shoot after taking a direct hit to the chest from an American soldier's M16 rifle[157].

After three days of ferocious fighting, the Northern forces finally began to retreat. Allied U.S. and South Vietnamese lost more than 600 men and suffered more than 2,000 wounded. Just when they thought it was over, on the way to the extraction point, the U.S. column was ambushed once more, and fighting ensued.

By the end of the fighting, 1 out of 4 members of the 7th Cavalry had been killed on the battlefield, some 234 soldiers. The People's Army had lost around 3,000 troops[158].

In the aftermath, Johnson immediately dispatched Secretary of Defence Robert McNamara to Saigon to establish what had happened. This visit turned out to be of monumental importance to McNamara. After seeing the devastation wreaked on the U.S. forces at the hand of the North Vietnamese first hand, he changed his opinion. He believed the U.S. could not win the war. He had seen enough; he wanted out[159].

William Westmoreland reached a different conclusion. He counted 12 communist deaths for every one American. He concluded this meant the U.S. could win a war of attrition in Vietnam. His logic was entirely flawed. At no point during the war did PAVN losses come close to the number of babies born in Northern Vietnam, so the North would always have a constant flow of soldiers ready to take up the mantle. Also, Westmoreland didn't consider how the loss of American life would affect public opinion in the U.S., and ultimately, how public opinion would influence U.S. policy in Vietnam[160].

On the other side of the country, Ho Chi Minh was doing some evaluating of his own. What he had seen at Ia Drang greatly encouraged him. The U.S., with all their technology, had not managed to overrun the communist forces. After seeing the U.S. battlefield strategies, the People's Army Commander Lt. Col. Nguyen Hu Anh developed the strategy that would win the war for the Northern Vietnamese. "Hug them by the belt buckle," as it was to be known, involved getting so close to the Americans that they couldn't use their artillery or aerial support without harming their troops[161].

The northern forces had also learned a valuable lesson in retreat. T U.S. would not chase the Vietnamese forces across the border

Cambodia. With that, Giap had found his winning formula. Get in close, strike hard, then retreat across a border.

More Troops

After the battle of Ia Drang, Westmoreland requested open-ended troop commitment from President Johnson. However, Johnson was unsure. The domestic backlash was already rumbling against the involvement of more troops; two young protesters had followed the Vietnamese Buddhist's lead and set themselves on fire in protest of the draft in early November. A march of more than 20,000 people had also joined a march on the White House protesting American involvement in Vietnam[162].

With most Americans favouring a ceasefire initiative in Vietnam, Johnson devised a plan to pause the bombing campaign in the North to give the North Vietnamese government another opportunity to engage in peace negotiations. On the 24th of December, Lyndon Johnson halted the bombing of the North for 37 days[163].

The pause was as much for the benefit of the American public and for the Johnson administration to appear as though they were attempting to broker peace, as it was for the actual pursuit of de-escalation. During the break, Johnson committed more troops to Vietnam, an indication of his commitment to de-escalation[164].

By 1966, flaws in the organisation of the American war effort were beginning to become apparent. The soldiers who had initially arrived at Danang in 1965 were starting to leave as troops arrived on 12-month tours. Once the soldiers had some experience under their belts and were beginning to understand the military situation in the country, they were removed and sent back to the U.S. This would severely hinder the American war effort. By contrast, the North Vietnamese fought until victory or death[165]. Seventy percent of all conflicts were initiated by the communist forces, indicating a war being fought on their terms, very much in the style and manner that suited them[166], against American soldiers who were withdrawn as soon as they accumulated significant battle experience.

Troop numbers and costs began to spiral. In 1965, Johnson's government had assumed the war effort would cost around $2 billion; its actual costs had been $8 billion. In 1966, the annual war effort would cost $21 billion, a significant increase. This was due to the escalation of the war on both sides.

Following the bombing break, Johnson extended the bombing targets in the North to include Hanoi and Haiphong and bombing intensified throughout the year. By 1967, 75% of the north's oil storage facilities lay in ruins, but there were still no fuel shortages. The U.S. was spending $10 for every $1 of damage inflicted on the North[167], yet Northern Vietnamese society continued, un-phased. Chinese supplies ensured the Northern communist government had ample weapons and ammunition and Chinese engineers rapidly rebuilt damaged infrastructure. The American bombing campaign was becoming an endless pit of spending, yielding minimal impact on Northern Vietnamese society.

In early 1966, the communists funnelled an additional 20,000 soldiers into the South. Nowhere in Southern Vietnam was secure. The search and destroy missions to root out the People's Army of Vietnam and the Vietcong were making more enemies than they were eliminating. Running out of ideas, Robert McNamara proposed the construction of an electronic fence across the 17th parallel, similar to the DMZ dividing North and South Korea. The fact that construction on the project began shows the extent the Johnson administration was grasping at straws to stem the 20 tons a day of supplies entering South Vietnam from the North. Shortly after the construction began, the absurdity of the project was realised and it was abandoned[168].

The Johnson administration was beginning to creak under the strain of the war. Divisions between the hawks and the doves were beginning to show publicly, and cracks were beginning to appear. The hawks of William Westmoreland, the Joint Chiefs of Staff and Walt Rostow were lobbying for unlimited U.S. commitment to the war. On the other side, Robert McNamara and the Pentagon had had enough of the war and very becoming very public in their desire for de-escalation and the implementation of troop number limits. Johnson navigated a route between the two, attempting to smooth over the cracks when they appeared[169]. But the hawks were winning the debate in Washington. At the end of 1966, almost 400,000 young American men were fighting for their lives in Southern Vietnam.

Chapter 7 – The Tet Nightmare

As 1967 rolled on, the hawks in Washington continued to exert more pressure on the President. In the Spring, Johnson announced the deployment of 45,000 more troops[170]. On August 9th, Johnson extended bombing targets. This time he allowed bombing to take place within the cities of Hanoi and Haiphong and included targets near the Chinese border. His aerial war would peak at this time, with 200 bombing flights launched over the north on August 20th, 1967, the most flights of any day in the whole war. The very next day two U.S. planes strayed into Chinese airspace and were shot down. Johnson was undoubtedly pushing his luck. While Johnson was warming to the idea of extending the war, attitudes among the public were beginning to freeze.

The extension of the draft call in 1966 had caused the ball of public backlash rolling, but 1967 was the year the anti-war movement spread in earnest. The draft was turning the Vietnam war into a "working class war[171]." The young men of America's more impoverished communities were being packed off to Vietnam and coming back in coffins draped with American flags, while University campuses across the country were full of young men from wealthy families, unhampered by the draft. Poor communities resented the privilege of draft evaders from prosperous communities, and the civil rights movement was gaining momentum as the African American population were disproportionately affected.

In 1967, figures in the public spotlight like Martin Luther King Jr. and Muhammed Ali were speaking out against the war[172]. In the middle of October, college students turned out to protest the draft during Stop the Draft Week. In cities across the country young men turned in their draft cards in the act of civil disobedience. This was a shock to Johnson. Many of these students were exempt from the draft. They were middle-class America, many of whom voted for Johnson.

To stop the tide of public opinion turning, Johnson pulled William Westmoreland home to give interviews and reassure the public America should still be involved in Vietnam. He knew the public couldn't publicly denounce a battle-hardened veteran fighting for his country. Westmoreland gave glowing reports on kill ratios and numbers of oil and ammunition depots destroyed across the television networks. He had the desired effect on Johnson's popularity. In December, after Westmoreland returned to the U.S., Johnson's public opinion polls rose by 11 points[173]. The public was even able to overlook that Le Duan's communist insurgents had dealt U.S. forces a significant blow and inflicted heavy casualties at Dak To. As 1967 rolled into 1968, Johnson stood on the deck of the *USS Enterprise* aircraft carrier and told the American people the war would continue "not many more nights[174]." Given what was to come in early 1968, Johnson was setting himself up for failure.

Johnson was becoming tired of McNamara's calls for troop limits. With the public turning against him, the last thing he wanted was a Secretary of Defence fuelling their concerns. McNamara was also a close friend of Bobby Kennedy, who was emerging as one of Johnson's political rivals for the Democratic 1968 presidential nomination. Johnson was becoming suspicious that McNamara would publicly double cross him and denounce his war strategy, thereby providing Bobby Kennedy with valuable ammunition in opposition[175]. Johnson could negotiate a job for McNamara as president of the World Bank. He would resign and take up the post in early 1968.

The Tet Offensive

Declassified documents from the Hanoi Politburo in 1967 indicate the communists had chosen 1968 as the year to make a significant impact on the war. They knew it was an election year and had seen the public becoming agitated with the war and Johnson's draft. They decided to launch a large-scale attack across the South in early 1968. The Vietcong guerrillas, supported by the People's Army of Vietnam, would attack every major city in Southern Vietnam. North Vietnamese Communist Party Chief, Le Duan outlined the Party's ultimate goals in a letter to the Southern fighters. He wanted "to shake the aggressive will of U.S. imperialism, compel it to change its strategy and de-escalate the war.[176]" Militarily, the attack was unsuccessful, but in terms of Le Duan's wider goals, the Tet offensive was an overwhelming victory for the Northern communists.

The Vietnamese holiday of Tet is one of the most significant annual celebrations within the country. Most Vietnamese spend it with their families. In the early hours of January 31st, the U.S. was utterly unprepared for a large-scale attack. In downtown Saigon, 200 colonels were at a party celebrating[177]. Despite the fact there were historical examples of the Vietnamese launching battles on their Tet holiday, they had used the holiday in 1789 to strike the Chinese forces during the war for independence[178], nobody in the White House or on the ground in Vietnam expected anything like what was about to occur.

In a display of impeccable organisation and synchronisation, Vietcong guerrillas and PAVN forces attacked all the major cities in Southern Vietnam. Thirteen of the 16 provincial capitals were hit[179]. In Saigon, Vietcong guerrillas blew a hole in the wall of the U.S. embassy, killed five American GIs and laid siege to the building[180]. In Hue, the communist forces took the Citadel and would hold it for a bloody 25 days.

In total 67,000 Vietcong and PAVN troops attacked more than 100 targets across the South[181]. In Saigon, 4,000 communist troops hit major sites across the city. In most cases, the uprising was crushed, and the Vietcong and Northern Communist forces were driven from the cities. Even in Hue, where the fighting was the most brutal, the communist forces eventually were forced to withdraw. But it came at a price. During the battles around Tet, the U.S. lost around 2,000 troops, and the ARVN sustained losses of around 4,000. This was a fraction of the 50,000 communists that died in the offensive[182], but despite the heavy communist losses, the Tet offensive had achieved its aims in the U.S.

The attack was even more impressive when you consider the level of planning undertaken by General Giap to give the offensive the highest possible chance of success. On the 21st of July, ten days before the attack, North Vietnamese forces attacked the rural American base of Khesanh. Despite its limited military significance, two to three divisions of North Vietnamese soldiers laid siege to the base to draw in U.S. troops out of the cities and set the stage for the Tet offensive. After eventually winning an intense battle between January and April 1968, the U.S. left the base abandoned when William Westmoreland ended his tour in June[183].

The Tet offensive pulled the war out of the rural countryside and showed the American people the communists had the capabilities of launching a major offensive across U.S. held cities. This was in direct contrast to the message President Johnson and the White House, who had been pedalling messages of imminent victory.

Images of the U.S. embassy in Saigon overrun with guerrillas raised questions about U.S. military competence at home. Images of a South Vietnamese policemen shooting a suspected Vietcong guerrilla in the head in a Saigon street also prompted questions about the conduct of the ARVN. The scenes broadcast straight into the homes of the American public showed total military disarray. This was when the grave reality of the situation dawned on the U.S. public. President Johnson had either been openly lying about the capabilities of communist forces, or he had drastically underestimated them. The reality is he was probably doing both.

The Tet Fallout

Primarily, Johnson wanted to mitigate the damages to public opinion. Rather than send William Westmoreland back to Vietnam to conduct a military response to Tet, he kept him in the U.S. to reassure the country of the progress of the war and ease their fears[184].

Influential journalist, Walter Cronkite had appeared on the news and openly called for ceasefire negotiations to end the Vietnam War. He represented the views of the general population. Johnson had put 500,000 Americans into Vietnam, he had lost 20,000 of them, and the public was now confronted with the harsh reality that this war could continue indefinitely. Ten thousand young American men could die year-after-year in Vietnam. Faced with the real costs of a sustained war in Vietnam, the public had no appetite for it. They wanted out.

For the communists, the Tet offensive had also taken its toll on the Vietcong. They had many more casualties than any other group and were the most heavily involved in the fighting. Communist agents from the North were sent south to rebuild the networks and restore the southern communist apparatus. But the southern Vietcong were not the same after Tet. They didn't get along with their Northern comrades and Tet represented the final stand for the Vietcong as a cohesive unit of southern communists[185].

The March 12th presidential primary in New Hampshire represented a litmus test to what extent the public still had faith in President Johnson. The primary went badly[186]. In a final attempt to bring the public back on side, Johnson announced another bombing halt to bring the communists to the negotiating table.

When his efforts failed, Johnson decided to pull out of the 1968 presidential race. He announced to the nation, "I shall not seek, and I will not accept the nomination of my party for another term as your president.[187]" The Vietnam war had become an all-encompassing quagmire that not even the President could escape.

Chapter 8 – Nixon and Kissinger

Before the curtain closed on Johnson's presidency, there was one final opportunity to salvage the wreck of Vietnam and bring peace under his leadership. After December 30th, 1967, the North warmed to the prospect of ceasefire negotiation. All they asked for, was a complete cessation of bombing targets north of the 17th parallel[188]. After Johnson withdrew from the presidential race, he began exploring the possibility of peace talks. His logic was that if he could bring peace to Vietnam, it might boost the popularity of the Democratic party in the run-up to the election and give Vice President, Hubert H. Humphrey a much-needed lift on the way into the polling stations.

For Republican candidate, Richard Nixon, this would have been disastrous. His whole campaign was built on the promise that if he got into the White House, he would bring an end to the war and be the one to negotiate peace. If Johnson did it first, it would take away his whole election platform[189]. Nixon had the lead going into the Autumn of 1968, but Humphrey was beginning to close the gap by the beginning of October. It was then that Richard Nixon received a phone call from Republican Advisor, Henry Kissinger. Kissinger informed Nixon that the USSR was pressuring Hanoi to agree to peace negotiations and if Johnson ceased the bombing, the prospect of peace before the November election looked likely.

The election was slipping away before Nixon's eyes. He knew the South Vietnamese president, Nguyen Van Thieu, feared Johnson selling them out in peace negotiations to bring a swift end to the war. Nixon decided to play on this and used one of his fundraisers, Anna Chennault, and Chinese businessman, Louis Kung, to convey to Thieu he would get a better peace deal once Nixon was in the White House. Nixon pressured Thieu to refuse any peace settlement that might bring a war to an end under President Johnson[190].

Johnson got wind of Richard Nixon's efforts to undermine his peace deal. He had the FBI follow Chennault and bug her phone and found she had spoken to South Vietnamese ambassador, Bui Diem. The bugged phones picked up her conversation. "Hold on. We are gonna win." She added, "please tell your boss to hold on.[191]"

Johnson couldn't go public with the limited evidence on hand, so he phoned Richard Nixon personally to confront him. In this conversation, and in all subsequent discussions both private and public, Nixon denied any involvement and proclaimed he had done nothing to undermine Johnson's talks.

In the end, Thieu refused to send his diplomats to Paris for the negotiations, bringing the whole discussion to a halt. Nixon went on to win the presidential election by just 1% of the vote, and the war would continue for another five years. A further 23,000 American lives were lost in Vietnam, and the peace negotiations Nixon and Kissinger brokered in 1973 was not out of reach to the Johnson administration in 1968[192].

Nixon's Campaign in Cambodia

Nixon didn't just play fast and loose with U.S. law in the election campaign. His whole presidency would become a string of illegal actions and cover-up campaigns.

Nixon was chosen by the American public because he had promised to de-escalate the war and bring their boys home. However, upon entering the Oval Office, Nixon believed he could increase the U.S. negotiating powers by disrupting the stream of supplies across the 17th parallel. Unlike Johnson before him, Nixon wanted to bomb targets in Cambodia, where he believed the North Vietnamese forces were routing their supplies to avoid American bombs[193]. On February 24th, 1969, Nixon began planning a bombing campaign in Cambodia that would be known as Operation Menu.

The operation had to be kept in total secrecy, even from Congress. They would never allow the bombing of a neutral country without a declaration of war. Also, if the American people found out the President they had elected to end the war was, in fact, expanding it, he would be crucified by the press. As a result, everything had to be approved by his personal National Security Advisor, Henry Kissinger. Kissinger selected every target himself and coordinated the flight times of every bombing raid. He entrusted General Creighton Adams with the destruction of every document which showed the target had been in Cambodia. Once the documents were destroyed, new ones were drawn up, replacing the Cambodian targets with new targets in Southern Vietnam[194].

Between 1969-1970, Kissinger coordinated 3,875 bombing raids on Cambodian soil, killing more than 100,000 civilians in an illegal extension of the war. But the bombs had no impact on the North Vietnamese supplies. All it did was destabilise Cambodia and ultimately create the conditions for the communist Khmer Rouge to seize control after the Vietnam war.

The 'Nixon Doctrine'

On July 25th, 1969, during a speech on the island of Guam, Nixon outlined exactly what his strategy would be regarding Vietnam. In what would become known as the 'Nixon Doctrine,' Richard Nixon outlined his policy of 'Vietnamization,' whereby the Vietnamese forces would gradually take over the brunt of the fighting[195]. He believed by getting the ARVN to take over the fighting with American equipment and aerial support; he could prevent a communist takeover the South.

The Nixon Doctrine was essentially a rebranding of Johnson's policies. Many in Johnson's office, including Robert McNamara, had had the same ideas about how to reduce American troop involvement in Vietnam. Nixon also didn't implement the policy straight away. He wanted to see how his bombing campaign in Cambodia would affect the war before he began implementing his policy of Vietnamization. This was precisely what Johnson had attempted to do. Bomb them into submission then negotiate a ceasefire[196].

Nixon had one trick up his sleeve to help bring the Northern Vietnamese government to the negotiating table. Borrowed from Eisenhower's approach to North Korea, Nixon wanted to make the North Vietnamese believe he was considering the use of atomic weapons in Vietnam. Calling it the "Madman theory," Nixon predicted that once Ho heard he was considering dropping nukes, Ho Chi Minh would "be in Paris in two days begging for peace.[197]"

But Nixon proved to be hopelessly wrong again. Why would Ho and the Viet Minh negotiate? Americans were already calling for troop withdrawals, and Nixon had to begin bringing boys home to make good his pre-election promises. The North Vietnamese knew without the help of American troops the South Vietnamese government would fall[198]; they just needed to be patient and bide their time. They also knew that the U.S. had far more to lose by deploying nuclear weapons than anyone else. With the public tide turning against the war, turning Vietnam into a nuclear crater would not save the South Vietnamese government or silence Nixon's critics[199].

Knowing that Nixon would never accept, the North Vietnamese government agreed to begin peace negotiations on the condition that Thieu's government resigned and a new government was created which would include Vietcong representation[200].

Rather than increasing his negotiating stock, the bombing of Cambodia was only proving that Nixon had no better ideas than his predecessor about how to secure a military victory in Vietnam. His negotiating stock fell even lower when, in early June, Nixon was forced to withdraw 25,000 troops to dull the roar of his critics. He also announced he would withdraw another 40,000 in September and reduce the drafts[201]. It bought him some time, but would not silence the critics for long.

On September 2nd, Ho Chi Minh died aged 79[202]. This was yet another blow to the American war effort. Le Duan, Pham Van Dong, and Vo Nguyen Giap had overseen the communist war strategy for many years. The loss of Ho would not impact the communist war machine. But it did make the Northern Vietnamese population even more determined to emerge victoriously. The war against the American occupiers had been Ho's struggle, and without him, his soldiers and people were more determined than ever to finish his life work.

The Anti-War Roar Becomes a Clamour

From the Autumn of 1969 to the Spring of 1970, the anti-war movement gained so much momentum; it appeared Nixon was losing control of the situation at home. On October 15th a series of moratoriums called by the anti-war movement led to strikes and protests at universities across the country. More than 200,000 people protested in Washington D.C[203].

Nixon needed to address the issue head-on. He knew he represented middle America and felt the anti-war protests were an assault on him from the left-wing intellectuals[204]. His approval ratings on the Vietnam issue were as high as 71%. So, on the 3rd of November, Nixon delivered his "silent majority" speech, where he appealed to his countrymen to unite for peace, "because North Vietnam cannot defeat or humiliate the United States. Only Americans can do that.[205]"

His words rang true. Just a few days later Seymour Hersh would break the story of the My Lai massacre, the world example of the whole war of American conduct humiliating the United States.

Seymour reported how in late 1968, William Calley and 100 soldiers from Charlie Company arrived in the small rural village of My Lai at around dawn. They had been tipped off there was a large contingent of Vietcong operating out of the village[206], but the scene that greeted them that morning was a sleepy agricultural hamlet enjoying their breakfast. The American public heard how Calley and his men had rounded up the villagers, raped women, burned houses and killed around 500 unarmed civilians. Eyewitness accounts described how the bodies were dumped in a ditch on the edge of the town, throwing grenades in amongst the bleeding mass of limbs. One small boy emerged from under the pile of bodies, having been shielded from the bullets and explosions. He ran crying from the scene, but Calley chased him and brought him back. He threw the boy into the ditch and shot him[207].

Bravo company carried out a similar attack on the nearby village of My Khe. In total, the massacre at the two villages left 504 Vietnamese civilians dead, including 182 women and 173 children[208]. Unsurprisingly, many of the villagers who survived the attack instantly joined the Vietcong in the fight against the Americans[209].

Calley went before a military court for his actions, but nobody else did. In 1971 he was convicted of murder, but Nixon intervened on his behalf and secured his release from prison three months later[210].

The revelation of American soldiers committing atrocities in Vietnam further soured public opinion to the war. The war had turned good American boys into murderers and savages. The public also soon realised it wasn't just the troops on the ground committing illegal acts. On April 30th, 1970, the press revealed Nixon's secret bombing campaign in Cambodia. With the cat out of the bag, Nixon saw no reason to hold back. He committed ground troops to Cambodia to root out PAVN bases along the border[211].

With Nixon's war unravelling before his very eyes, protests began again in earnest on college campuses. Four days after the news of

Operation Menu going public, in Akron Ohio, the Ohio National Guard fired at student protestors 67 times. They killed four students and paralysed another[212]. Nixon was losing his grasp on the war. It was time to begin negotiating.

The Beginning of the End

On February 21st, 1970, Henry Kissinger secretly met with Le Duc Tho, the North Vietnamese delegate, in Paris. The meeting would be the first of many in a peace process that would span three years. There were official channels of negotiations, but both Nixon and Kissinger preferred clandestine meetings away from the prying eyes of the media. By conducting peace negotiations behind closed doors, the cunning pair could exclude Secretary of State William Rogers and Defence Secretary Melvin Laird. They could also keep Thieu out of the picture, who would never agree to any settlement that might leave the South Vietnamese government in a disadvantaged position[213].

This also suited Hanoi. They saw the negotiations as a way to divide the U.S. from their Southern Vietnamese allies. Kissinger preferred to conduct the negotiations away from the prying eyes of the American press. He could leak snippets of information to publications and journalists he liked and trusted, but he could exercise strict control over what the information the American public had access to[214].

The peace negotiations in 1970 produced limited results. Le Duc Tho had to run every agreement past the government in Hanoi, which slowed the whole process. He often arrived at the negotiations with a headache. When he was in one of these moods, Kissinger and his delegation knew no progress would be made that day[215].

But Le Duc Tho and the North Vietnamese had no reason to rush. Public support for the war was tumbling and every troop withdrawal the public forced Nixon to make, reduced the US's bargaining power. With protests at campuses across the US becoming a weekly occurrence, Nixon withdrew American combat troops from Cambodia in late 1970[216]. It was clear the US military campaign would not secure them more favourable negotiating conditions on the battlefield. It would fall on Kissinger to negotiate the best deal he could under the existing stalemate.

Although Kissinger had relative freedom over the negotiations, Hanoi was adamant that a deal had to include the resignation of the Saigon government and formation of a new coalition government. This was beyond what Kissinger could accept. Nixon had entrusted Kissinger to secure "peace with honour," and any agreement which brought communists into the South Vietnamese government could not be spun to the American public as honourable.

By the end of 1970, American troop numbers were down to just 280,000, and the ARVN was struggling to compensate for the departing U.S. troops. They had been taught under the guidance of U.S. military advisers since the '50s, but the methods they had learned were conventional warfare methods, totally unsuitable for the guerrilla tactics employed by the communists[217]. In early 1971, General Haig travelled to Vietnam to assess the situation. His conclusions were far from encouraging. Haig described Thieu's soldier's battlefield strategy as a retreat "in an orderly and tactically sound fashion.[218]"

The situation at home was reaching new depths. William Scranton described the division in American society "as deep as any since the Civil War.[219]" Things were about to get worse. In 1971, the Pentagon Papers outlining a governmental policy on Vietnam from 1945 to 1967. The papers showed the public the government's scepticism that military escalation would yield results and the extreme lengths the Johnson administration had gone to persuade the public progress was being made in Vietnam[220]. This turned more people at home against the war. They had been deceived about escalation, lied to about the war progress, and now they had a president that had escalated the war rather than bring it to a swift conclusion.

Friction was also emerging between the American GIs still based in Saigon and the ARVN. As American troops were flying home in their thousands throughout 1970 and 1971, the South Vietnamese population began to resent their American guests. They saw the withdrawal of troops as the U.S. leaving South Vietnam to its fate. Small arguments between GIs and ARVN troops over bumped cars and equipment quickly began escalating into a confrontation[221].

The Road to Peace Lay Through China

With the peace negotiation getting nowhere, and the U.S. forces in Vietnam numbering around 140,000, Kissinger and Nixon needed to devise a new strategy to advance the peace talks in Paris.

Hanoi had depended on Soviet weapons and ammunition since the start of the war, and Chinese rice kept their population fed while they threw all their resources at the war effort. At the start of 1972, an opportunity presented itself for Henry Kissinger to use shifting Sino-Soviet relations to pressure the Northern Vietnamese into a peace deal.

The opportunity to thaw relations with China presented itself as the Sino-Soviet relationship was under strain due to a border dispute and Chinese interference with the Soviet supply chain to Northern Vietnam through China[222]. Henry Kissinger embarked on a secret visit to China in 1971, but it wasn't until Nixon's visit the following year significant progress could be made in normalising Sino-American relations.

To fend off the rising Soviet threat, Mao Zedong warmed to the idea of reconciliation with the United States. This would be a nightmare scenario for Hanoi. If Beijing and Washington forged friendly ties and the Chinese government stopped providing Hanoi with assistance to unify Vietnam, the North Vietnamese would be forced to abandon the struggle. Nixon arrived in Beijing on February 21st, 1972, determined to make a deal with Mao. He got his wish. Mao agreed to pressure

Hanoi into making peace with the U.S., providing the United States removed their troops from Taiwan[223].

But Nixon would have to wait a little longer for peace. Faced with the prospect of being coerced by the Chinese to sign a peace deal, Hanoi launched one final push to achieve unification in Vietnam by military means. In the Spring of 1972, Hanoi launched its final offensive from its base in Laos and Cambodia. The offensive failed to end the military and political stalemate, and in response, Nixon launched an intense bombing campaign across the North[224]. The next time Hanoi came to the negotiating table in Paris, they would have a different approach to compromising.

In 1972, the U.S. demands at the Paris meetings centred on the immediate return of all U.S. prisoners of war and a ceasefire that would end the fighting in Vietnam, and extend across Cambodia and Laos. The Northern Vietnamese delegate returned to the negotiations in the Summer and Autumn of 1972 ready to accept that Thieu's government would not be disbanded[225]. They also wanted U.S. assurances they would receive aid in the rebuilding of their cities and towns that had been destroyed by U.S. bombing raids.

Once the communist government dropped their insistence on the formation of a coalition government, an agreement could be reached relatively quickly. By October, Kissinger and Le Duc Tho had an agreement drawn up and ready to present to their respective governments[226].

How Do You Solve a Problem like Thieu?

Nixon immediately gave his approval, all that remained was a trip to Saigon to get Thieu on board. In mid-October 1972, Kissinger had the unenvious task of presenting the agreement to Thieu and persuading him why it would be in the Southern Vietnamese interests to sign the agreement. Kissinger assured Thieu if the North broke the ceasefire and attempted to reunify Vietnam through military means once the

Americans had left, the U.S. Air Force would immediately resume heavy bombing in the North. He also promised Thieu's government an injection of aid before the agreement was signed so the Southern regime would be in the strongest position possible once it came into effect[227].

Thieu was furious. He felt misled and betrayed by the Americans and felt his exclusion from the peace talks had been a deliberate attempt to negotiate for South Vietnam behind his back. He felt the Americans were forcing an agreement on the South Vietnamese people without any thought for their needs and desires. His main grievance was with the notion that communist forces would be permitted to stay in the South, but he had minor issues with almost every point on the agreement, including the wording which he found weak[228].

Rather than go back to Paris and rehash Thieu's amendments with the North Vietnamese delegation, Nixon and Kissinger told the North Vietnamese government to wait. They thought they could persuade Thieu into accepting the agreement. The government in Hanoi interpreted the move as an indication the U.S. was backing out of the agreement and they released press statements blasting Nixon's government[229].

Kissinger and his delegation returned to the negotiating table in Paris in November. The North Vietnamese delegation had abandoned their compromising stance and instead wanted to take back many of their initial concessions. Having come so close to a ceasefire agreement, Kissinger could see all the progress he had made since 1970 unravelling before his very eyes. The negotiations collapsed on December 13th.

Nixon was livid. He immediately planned operation Line-backer II, a vast bombing campaign designed to show Hanoi precisely what would happen if they allowed peace negotiations to collapse. Between December 18th and 29th, American planes dropped 20,000 tons of bombs on Hanoi and Haiphong, killing more than 1,600 civilians.

Nixon only ended the bombing because Hanoi agreed to resume peace talks[230].

Once peace talks resumed in January, things progressed much faster. The communists stopped introducing new demands, and the October agreement was reworked with minimal modifications. The agreement was drawn up and finalised on January 23rd[231], amid toasting and celebrations. But once more, the U.S. still had to get Thieu to agree.

This time, Nixon himself wanted to stress to Theiu this was the end of the road. He wrote Thieu a series of tough letters in which he emphasised the U.S. had negotiated the best deal it possibly could. He told the Saigon regime this was it; the U.S. had given every drop of blood it could. He reassured Thieu the U.S. would continue to support the Saigon government, but that Thieu needed to get on board with this agreement. Thieu reluctantly accepted, allowing Secretary of State William Rogers to fly to Paris and sign the agreement into effect on January 27th, 1973.

Withdrawal

Nixon released a statement to the public celebrating his achievement of the "goal of peace with honour in Vietnam[232]." The last American troops left Vietnam on March 29th, and Hanoi returned the last American prisoner of war on March 29th[233]. Congress stopped the bombing of Cambodia on August 14th,[234] and one would be forgiven for suspecting the whole miserable conflict of Vietnam was over. Unfortunately, the final ending of the Vietnam era wasn't to come for another two years.

The ceasefire agreement would ultimately break down. Within a few months of inking the ceasefire agreement, the communists were already testing the water with some armed skirmishes. But on the side of the U.S., it also failed to honour its commitments. Hanoi never received any of the economic aid it was promised under the Paris agreements. When the communists began to launch small attacks once more in the South, congress essentially cut off military and economic aid to the South Vietnamese government. The U.S. had failed to honour any of its aid commitments to either the Northern or Southern governments[235].

In 1974, Thieu tells the U.S. government war has begun again and by June, the communists are increasing the flow of men and supplies to the South once more. By September, Hanoi drew up plans to renew fighting.

Throughout 1975, without any U.S. assistance, South Vietnam collapsed to the invading communists. Beginning with Phuoc Long province in January, the North Vietnamese gradually moved south, taking Southern cities and provinces. Hue fell in late March and on April 30th, communist forces seized Saigon[236].

It is impossible to know if the outcome would have been different had the U.S. given both sides their promised aid, but in withdrawing it, the U.S. had sealed Vietnam's fate.

Conclusion

America's failings in Vietnam, remain something of an enigma. How did the world's military superpower come unstuck against a small backward Southeast Asian military force? So much so, the country would fall under communist control within two years of American troops withdrawing. The U.S. invested 56,000 lives and more than $141 billion[237], yet still could not prevent the inevitable.

Part of the problem lay with the attitude of the American Presidents towards Vietnam. Nobody wanted to lose the war, but nobody wanted to fight an unlimited war either, out of fear of Chinese intervention or public backlash at home. Johnson limited his aerial war and Nixon could not openly be seen committing more U.S. resources to ensure an American victory.

The other issue was the Americans never fully understood the nuances of Vietnam. As early on as the 1950s under Ngo Dinh Diem, the U.S. failed to understand how his removal would undermine the whole Saigon regime. Johnson's Rolling Thunder campaign was ineffective due to a complete misunderstanding of how the Northern Vietnamese operated their supply lines and organised their military command in the battlefield. The search and destroy missions actively drove rural communities to expand the Vietcong ranks, and Westmoreland's obsession will kill counts and statistics gave an entirely inaccurate representation of the progression of the war.

The U.S. also failed to make any headway with the North Vietnamese communist allies. It wasn't until 1971 the avenue of cooperating with China was explored, and it yielded significant results in the peace negotiations. Had the American's explored this avenue earlier and found an arrangement to limit Sino-Soviet assistance to Northern Vietnam, the Hanoi regime would have been strangled to the negotiating table. Also, had the American's not have provided so much assistance to the South Vietnamese, China and the Soviet Union would have provided less support to the North, and the Vietnamese Civil War could have played out quietly on its own, without the involvement of the world's superpowers.

Vietnam's Legacy

American failings didn't just occur during the Vietnam era. More American war veterans have committed suicide since the Vietnam war than died in the conflict itself. The spectre of the Vietnam War haunted the American psyche for decades after the last troops returned home. GIs struggled with drug addiction and post-traumatic stress disorder as they tried to make sense of the conflict their government had them participate in.

This pales in comparison to the war's legacy on the Vietnamese population. Babies born with deformities caused by defoliant chemicals sprayed on the population plagued the Vietnamese population in the post-war years. The war claimed 1.35 million lives, the bulk of which were civilians. Almost every family in the country had lost someone and were forced to begin reconstructing their country and their livelihoods.

Aspects of the Vietnam War have also been used in global conflicts since. The Tet offensive was replicated by the Iraqi insurgency movement in Baghdad, to some degrees of success and Donald Trump is employing his variation of Nixon's "madman" approach, suggesting his finger may be hovering over the nuclear button.

The Vietnam War was a civil war, a colonial war, a nationalist struggle, and an international conflict. Along with its Korean counterpart, it represented a chapter in Cold War history, but also a standalone war with its roots entrenched in the years of the French occupation. It forced the U.S. to confront its limitations in a way no conflict had ever done, and its effects of the war continue to ripple across American society today.

More than four decades later, and historians continue to grapple with the complex topic of the Vietnam War. Each declassified document offers a seemingly new perspective on the conflict, reworking our understanding of the era repeatedly. New interpretations will emerge, but the full historical impact of the Vietnam War cannot be overstated.

Preview of World War 2

A Captivating Guide from Beginning to End

Introduction

The Second World War was one of the most traumatic events in human history. Across the world, existing conflicts became connected, entangling nations in a vast web of violence. It was fought on land, sea, and air, touching every inhabited continent. Over 55 million people died, some of them combatants, some civilians caught up in the violence, and some murdered by their own governments.

It was the war that unleashed the Holocaust and the atomic bomb upon the world. But it was also a war that featured acts of courage and self-sacrifice on every side.

The world would never be the same again.

Chapter 1 – The Rising Tide

The Second World War grew out of conflicts in two parts of the world: Europe and East Asia. Though the two would eventually become entangled, it's easier to understand the causes of the war by looking at them separately.

Europe's problems were rooted in centuries of competition between powerful nations crammed together on a small and densely populated continent. Most of the world's toughest, most stubborn, and most ambitious kids were crammed together in a single small playground. Conflict was all but inevitable.

The most recent large European conflict had been the First World War. This was the first industrialized war, a hugely traumatic event for all the participants. In the aftermath, Germany was severely punished for its aggression by the victorious Allied powers. The remains of the Austro-Hungarian empire fell apart, creating instability in the east. And the Russian Empire, whose government had been overthrown during the turmoil of the war, became the Union of Soviet Socialist Republics (USSR), the first global power to adopt the new ideology of communism.

From this situation of instability, a new form of politics emerged. Across Europe, extreme right-wing parties adopted ultra-nationalistic views. Many of them incorporated ideas of racial superiority. Most were strongly influenced by the fear of communism. All relied on scapegoating outsiders to make themselves more powerful.

The first to reach prominence was the Fascist Party in Italy under Benito Mussolini. Mussolini was a veteran soldier, gifted orator, and skilled administrator. He rallied disenchanted left-wingers and those who felt put down by corrupt politicians and forceful trade unions. Using a mixture of persuasion and intimidation, he won the 1922 election and became prime minister. Through a series of laws, he turned his country into a one-party dictatorship. Most of his achievements were domestic, bringing order and efficiency at the price of freedom, but he also had ambitions abroad. He wanted Italy to be a colonial power like Britain or France, and so in 1935-6 his forces conquered Abyssinia.

Mussolini was surpassed in almost every way by the man who reached power in Germany a decade later—Adolph Hitler. A decorated veteran of the First World War, Hitler was embittered at the Versailles Treaty, which imposed crushing restrictions upon Germany in the aftermath of the war. He developed a monstrous ideology that combined racism, homophobia, and a bitter hatred of communism. Like Mussolini, he brought together oratory and street violence to seize control of Germany. Once elected chancellor in 1933, he purged all opposition and had himself made Führer, the nation's "leader" or "guide." He then escalated the rearmament of Germany, casting off the shackles of Versailles.

Hitler and Mussolini intervened in the Spanish Civil War of 1936-9. Rather than have their nations join the war, they sent parts of their armed forces to support Franco's right-wing armies, testing new military technology and tactics while ensuring the victory of a man they expected to be an ally—a man who would in fact keep his nation out of the coming war for Europe.

Meanwhile, Hitler was playing a game of chicken with the other European powers. In March 1936, he occupied the Rhineland, a part of Germany that had been demilitarized after the war. Two years later, he annexed his own homeland of Austria, with its large German-speaking population. He occupied parts of Czechoslovakia that fall and finished the job off the following spring. At every turn, the rest of Europe backed down rather than go to war to protect less powerful nations.

Meanwhile, in Asia, the Chinese revolutions of 1911 and 1913, along with the Chinese Civil War that broke out in 1927, had triggered a parallel period of instability. Nationalists and communists battled for control of a vast nation, destroying the regional balance of power.

Japan was a nation on the rise. Economic growth had created a sense of ambition which had then been threatened by a downturn in the 1930s. Interventions by Western powers, including their colonies in Asia and a restrictive naval treaty of 1930, embittered many in Japan, who saw the Europeans and Americans as colonialist outsiders meddling in their part of the world.

The Japanese began a period of expansion, looking to increase their political dominance and their control of valuable raw resources. They invaded Chinese Manchuria in 1931 and from then on kept encroaching on Chinese territory. At last, in 1937, the Chinese nationalist leader Chiang Kai-Shek gave up on his previous policy of giving ground to buy himself time. A minor skirmish escalated into the Second Sino-Japanese War.

From an Asian point of view, the war had already begun. But it would be Hitler who pushed Europe over the brink and gave the war its Western start date of 1939.

Check out this book!

Preview of Maya Civilization
A Captivating Guide to Maya History and Maya Mythology

Introduction

You've probably heard of the Maya and their astounding civilization before. You may recognize the famous Maya calendar that apparently predicted a worldwide apocalypse back in 2012. The media were quick to jump on board this mind-boggling prophecy (which we'll debunk later in this book). Newspapers and websites were filled with stories of doomsday that failed to materialize. Lucky for us, we did wake up on December 22, 2012, when the Maya calendar apparently ended.

But what you may not know is how much the Maya legacy is impacting your life today. Do you love to treat yourself to a frothy hot chocolate before bed, or indulge in an after-dinner chocolate treat? Do you love adding a side of fries to your meal? What about tomatoes for your favorite Italian dishes? If you do, you may not be aware that you have the Maya and the Spanish conquistadors to thank, for they introduced these goods to Europe and other continents.

But Maya are far more than just their food. In this captivating guide, you'll discover why Maya have gained such worldwide admiration over the many other civilizations that existed in Mesoamerica at the time. You'll learn how the Maya civilization developed, the major turning points in their 3,000-year-long history, the mysteries surrounding their demise, and some of the unique places where Maya exist to this day.

Oh yes. If you think the Maya are gone, think again. As opposed to popular belief, the Maya are neither extinct, nor quiet. They are six-million strong, according to some sources, most of them living in Guatemala. What's more, in 1994 one of the surviving Maya tribes, the Zapatistas, launched a rebellion in southeast Mexico against global trade and capitalism.

In the first part of this book, we'll first examine the origins of the Maya civilization and the Mesoamerican cultures that may have influenced them. We'll discuss why Maya (out of all the different tribes that existed in the region at the time) have captured the imagination of the West so much. We'll look at how they lived, ate, slept, whom they worshipped, and how they used herbal medicines and hallucinogenic plants to treat the sick.

We'll look at their trading routes and rivalries with another famous Mesoamerican tribe—the Aztecs. We'll look into the decline of the Maya civilization and how their rivalries with the Aztecs aided the victory of the Spanish conquistadors in the 16th century, led by the famous Spaniard Hernán Cortés. We won't forget to mention the heroic efforts of the Maya to fend off the Spaniards, and why they were able to succeed at this task for much longer than the Aztecs. We'll even track down the Maya living today, a population that is still six-million strong and adhere to many of the traditions that their ancestors once held. In among the battle tales and gore of human sacrifice, we'll look at some delicious cocoa recipes, Maya-style, that you can make at home.

After we've learnt all about the Maya origins, their cuisine, and their most notable events to present day, we'll delve into the aspect that's often the reason why so many people have been fascinated by the Maya civilization throughout the ages. We will look at their mythology, cosmology, and the solar calendar that resulted in the infamous doomsday scare back in 2012.

So buckle up and get ready to be transported to the warm and wet plains of the Maya civilization—it will be a journey you'll never forget.

Maya Timeline

The Archaic Period:
- 7000 to 2000 BC

The Preclassic Period:
- Early Preclassic – 2000 to 1000 BC
- Middle Preclassic – 1000 to 300 BC
- Late Preclassic – 300 BC to AD 250

The Classic Period:
- Early Classic – AD 250 to 600
- Late Classic – AD 600 to 900
- Terminal Classic – AD 900 to 1000

The Postclassic Period:
- Early Postclassic – AD 1000 to 1250
- Late Postclassic – AD 1250 to 1521
- The Spanish Invasion – AD 1521

Glossary of Important Maya Terms

- Cacao – the seeds that the Maya used in order to create their delicious cacao drink, also known as "bitter water."
- Cenote – a type of sink-hole that the Maya used to get fresh supplies of water (and to perform ritual sacrifice).
- Conquistadors – the Spanish military leaders who led the conquest of America in the 16th century, including Hernándo Cortés.
- The Dresden Codex – located in a museum in Germany, the Dresden Codex is one of the oldest surviving books from the

Americas. It contains 78 pages with important information on rituals, calculations, and the planetary movements of Venus.
- Haab – one of the several Maya calendars (this one measured time in 365-day cycles).
- Hero Twins – the central characters in the Maya creation story and the ancestors of future Maya rulers.
- Huipil – traditional dress for Maya women.
- Maize – the staple food of Maya civilization, an ancient form of corn (the Maize god was one of the most important deities for Maya).
- Mesoamerica – this is what we call the region of the Americas before the arrival of the Spanish fleets and its colonisation in the 15th and 16th centuries.
- Popol Vuh – the story of creation of the world that was passed down from generation to generation (it was recorded by the Quiche Maya who lived in the region of modern day Guatemala).
- Shamanism – an important spiritual practice throughout Mesoamerica (during shamanic trance a shaman would be able to practice divination and healing).
- Stelae – an upright stone slab or column, often used as a gravestone. These structures usually contained commemorative inscriptions.
- Yucatan Peninsula – a region in the southeast of Mexico, where some of the Maya civilization developed, especially in the Postclassic period.

Part 1 – History

Chapter 1: The Origins of the Mesoamerican Civilizations

Maya have captivated the imagination of the West ever since their culture was "discovered" in the 1840s by the American writer and explorer John Lloyd Stephens and the English artist and architect Frederick Catherwood. The latter is best known for his intricate and detailed images of the Maya ruins that he and Stephens later published in their book *Incidents of Travel in Central America*.

But just because the West didn't discover the Maya until the mid-nineteenth century doesn't mean that they lived in obscurity the rest of the time. In fact, their history is rich with fantastical tales and splendour and a diet that people living in other regions at the time could only dream about. The origins of the Maya civilization can be traced all the way back to 7,000 BC.

The Archaic period: 7000 – 2000 BC

People were once hunter-gatherers, living a largely nomadic lifestyle, according to the whims of nature and the sharp-toothed animals all around them. They had to keep moving in order to stay safe and keep up their food supplies. But in 7000 BC a new shift began—the hunter-gatherers who lived in Mesoamerica discovered something that would change their region forever. They began planting crops.

It's not entirely clear why this shift occurred when it did. The changing weather patterns may have had something to do with it—the climate gradually became wetter and warmer, so many of the larger animals that the Mesoamericans relied on for food became extinct. As a result, they had to eat more plants and grains, so eventually they started growing some for themselves. They used many techniques to make their lands more fertile. For example, they discovered that burning trees helped put nitrates into the soil to make it more fertile. (Don't try this at home.)

As a result, these ancient people started having a much more varied diet. We know this thanks to the discoveries by the archaeologists working in the Tehuacan Valley of Mexico, a site that contains the best evidence for human activity in the Archaic time period in Mesoamerica. The locals were able to plant and eat things that we often take for granted today, such as peppers, squash, and avocado. Not to mention early forms of corn, the grain that would become the staple food in Mesoamerica.

Since they were able to grow the food that they needed in order to survive, these ancient people no longer needed to move around as much. They began settling down into small villages, leading to the first known settlements in Mesoamerica. The first evidence of individual burial spots directly under people's homes dates back to 2600 BC. These early settlements included temples and sacred spots for worship, suggesting an early form of a civilization. Temples, worship, and sacrifice remained a prominent theme throughout the Maya history, and we'll cover more of it later.

But the Maya did not evolve in a vacuum. There were many cultures and tribes that existed around them, and each had some influence on their culture, customs, and civilization. We'll examine these, one at a time, as we travel through time to really appreciate the interplay between those cultures and the Maya. Before we go onto learning about how these early settlements evolved into the Maya civilization, let's look at one of the most important tribes that existed in Mesoamerica at the time—the Olmecs.

The Olmecs: 1,200 – 300 BC

No one really knows where the Olmecs came from or where they disappeared to. But their legacy on the Mesoamerican tribes, including the Maya, is huge.

The Olmecs inhabited the area along the Gulf of Mexico, and their impressive stone cities gave way to myths about giants who may have lived in this area at the time. The Olmec craftsmanship was highly sophisticated—there are some impressive sculptures that survive to this day as evidence of their superb skills.

Sometimes ancient history is a bit of guesswork, leaving you to fill in the gaps left out by missing evidence. It's interesting that there's a total lack of battle scenes in the Olmec art—something that most other cultures are quick to display in their monuments and sculptures. The fact that they depict no battle scenes could mean one of two things. Either they did not engage in any war conflict, or they simply didn't feel like showing off about it. You decide.

Until recently, the Olmecs were regarded as the "mother culture" of all the great Mesoamerican civilizations to come, including the Maya and the Aztecs. But more recent sources argue that the Maya actually had a counter-influence on the Olmecs.

When it comes to the Olmec mythology, displayed in their surviving temples and sculptures, there are definite traces of shamanic practice. Many of their sculptures depict a were-jaguar, a core element of shamanism, symbolizing shamanic trance. The Maya saw the jaguar as a transformational animal, who feels at home at night-time, a symbol for the Underworld. The symbolism of shamanistic practice is present in all later Mesoamerican cultures, including the Maya.

The Olmecs may have had an important motif of a twin deity, that may have influenced the mythology of the Maya Hero Twins. The Hero Twins is a way to express the duality that the Maya saw around them—the complementary duality between day and night, life and death, the masculine and the feminine. The Olmec flaming eyebrows, the first corn, and cross bands are all symbols that would later appear in the Maya art, connected to astrology. Ancestor worship was also prevalent in the Olmec tradition, as it was later in the Maya and most Mesoamerican cultures at the time.

Challenge your perceptions—Dwarfism

When studying ancient history and learning about cultures, it's always interesting to find out what light it can shed on the culture that we inhabit today. Sometimes the things that we perceive as true are to do with our cultural upbringing. For example, nowadays we define people who are born with smaller organisms and don't grow much taller than 147cm as having the medical condition of Dwarfism or "short stature." We tend to see this as an abnormality, assuming that people born with this condition would face certain limitations in life.

Well, the Olmec also saw Dwarfism as an abnormality, only not a limiting one. In fact, it was quite the opposite. As the director of the Maya Exploration Center, Dr. Edwin Barnhart explains in his audio-lecture series *Maya To Aztec: Ancient Mesoamerica Revealed* that if you were born with a very small organism in the Olmec or the later Maya culture, you'd be seen as a magical being, touched by the gods. You'd be enjoying all kinds of luxuries, often appearing in the king's court. This may be something to do with their belief that the sky was held up by four dwarves, and so they gave them special treatment.

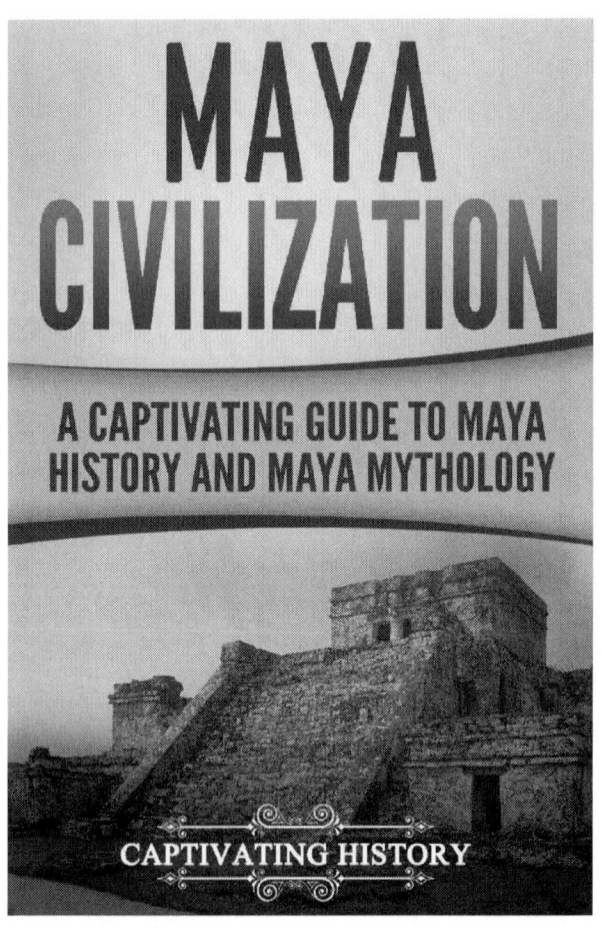

Check out this book!

Free Bonus from Captivating History (Available for a Limited time)

Hi History Lovers!

Now you have a chance to join our exclusive history list so you can get your first history ebook for free as well as discounts and a potential to get more history books for free! Simply visit the link below to join.

Captivatinghistory.com/ebook

Also, make sure to follow us on:

Twitter: @Captivhistory

Facebook: Captivating History: @captivatinghistory

Sources

[1] Karnow, Stanley, *Vietnam: A History*, (Middlesex: Penguin, 1984), p.106

[2] Logevall, Fredrik, *The Origins of the Vietnam War*, (New York: Routledge, 2013), p.8

[3] Ibid. p.7

[4] Karnow, Stanley, *Vietnam: A History*, (Middlesex: Penguin, 1984), p.113

[5] Ibid. p.115

[6] Ibid. p.113

[7] Karnow, Stanley, *Vietnam: A History*, (Middlesex: Penguin, 1984), p.117

[8] Ibid. p.114

[9] Logevall, Fredrik, *The Origins of the Vietnam War*, (New York: Routledge, 2013), p.8

[10] Ibid.

[11] Ibid. p.114

[12] Ibid. p.109

[13] Ibid.

[14] Ibid. pp118-119

[15] Ibid. p.122

[16] Ibid.

[17] Ibid. p.123

[18] Ibid. p.124

[19] Ibid. p.125

[20] Logevall, Fredrik, *The Origins of the Vietnam War*, (New York: Routledge, 2013), p.12

[21] Tonnesson, Stein, 'The Longest Wars: Indochina 1945-76', *Journal of Peace Research*, 22, 1 (1985), p.10

[22] Karnow, Stanley, *Vietnam: A History*, (Middlesex: Penguin, 1984), p.126

[23] Ibid. p.127

[24] Tonnesson, Stein, 'The Longest Wars: Indochina 1945-76', *Journal of Peace Research*, 22, 1 (1985), p.11

[25] Ibid.

[26] Ibid.

[27] Karnow, Stanley, *Vietnam: A History*, (Middlesex: Penguin, 1984), p.146

[28] Ibid.

[29] Ibid. p.147

[30] Ibid. p.149

[31] Logevall, Fredrik, *The Origins of the Vietnam War*, (New York: Routledge, 2013), p.15

[32] Tonnesson, Stein, 'The Longest Wars: Indochina 1945-76', *Journal of Peace Research*, 22, 1 (1985), p.12

[33] Ibid.

[34] Logevall, Fredrik, *The Origins of the Vietnam War*, (New York: Routledge, 2013), p.15

[35] Ibid.

[36] Tonnesson, Stein, 'The Longest Wars: Indochina 1945-76', *Journal of Peace Research*, 22, 1 (1985), p.13

[37] Ibid. p.16

[38] Ibid. p.13

[39] Ibid. p.14

[40] Ibid. p.14

[41] Fifield, Russel H., 'The Thirty Years War in Indochina: A Conceptual Framework', *Asian Survey*, 17, 9, (1977), p.861

[42] Karnow, Stanley, *Vietnam: A History*, (Middlesex: Penguin, 1984), p.160

[43] Fifield, Russel H., 'The Thirty Years War in Indochina: A Conceptual Framework', *Asian Survey*, 17, 9, (1977), p.861

[44] Karnow, Stanley, *Vietnam: A History*, (Middlesex: Penguin, 1984), p.173

[45] Ibid. p.175

[4646] Logevall, Fredrik, *The Origins of the Vietnam War*, (New York: Routledge, 2013), p.17

[47] Logevall, Fredrik, *The Origins of the Vietnam War*, (New York: Routledge, 2013), p.17

[48] Fifield, Russel H., 'The Thirty Years War in Indochina: A Conceptual Framework', *Asian Survey*, 17, 9, (1977), p.863

[49] Karnow, Stanley, *Vietnam: A History*, (Middlesex: Penguin, 1984), p.190

[50] Ibid. p.191

[51] Ibid. p.196

[52] Ibid. p.197

[53] Ibid. p.193

54 Tonnesson, Stein, 'The Longest Wars: Indochina 1945-76', *Journal of Peace Research*, 22, 1 (1985), p.25

55 Ibid. p.26

56 O'Connell, Chuck, 'Ideology as History: A Critical Commentary on Burns and Novick's "The Vietnam War"', *City Watch*, 25 Sep, 2017, Available at <http://www.citywatchla.com/index.php/important-reads-for-rss/14067-ideology-as-history-a-critical-commentary-on-burns-and-novick-s-the-vietnam-war>, [Accessed on 26 Sep 2017]

57 Tonnesson, Stein, 'The Longest Wars: Indochina 1945-76', *Journal of Peace Research*, 22, 1 (1985), p.26

58 Karnow, Stanley, *Vietnam: A History*, (Middlesex: Penguin, 1984), p.217

59 Ibid. p.213

60 Ibid. p.214

61 Jacobs, Seth, *America's Middle Man in Vietnam: Ngo Dinh Diem, Religion, Race and U.S Intervention in Southeast Asia, 1950-1957*, (Durham NC, Duke University Press, 2004), pp.12-13

62 O'Connell, Chuck, 'Ideology as History: A Critical Commentary on Burns and Novick's "The Vietnam War"', *City Watch*, 25 Sep, 2017, Available at <http://www.citywatchla.com/index.php/important-reads-for-rss/14067-ideology-as-history-a-critical-commentary-on-burns-and-novick-s-the-vietnam-war>, [Accessed on 26 Sep 2017]

63 O'Connell, Chuck, 'Ideology as History: A Critical Commentary on Burns and Novick's "The Vietnam War"', *City Watch*, 25 Sep, 2017, Available at <http://www.citywatchla.com/index.php/important-reads-for-rss/14067-ideology-as-history-a-critical-commentary-on-burns-and-novick-s-the-vietnam-war>, [Accessed on 26 Sep 2017]

64 Ibid.

65 Ibid.

66 Ibid.

[67] Ibid.

[68] Ibid.

[69] Karnow, Stanley, *Vietnam: A History*, (Middlesex: Penguin, 1984), p.222

[70] Ibid. p.223

[71] Ibid.

[72] Ibid.

[73] Fisher, James T., 'The Second Catholic President: Ngo Dinh Diem, John F. Kennedy, and the Vietnam Lobby, 1954-1963', *U.S Catholic Historian*, 15, 3, (1997), p.19

[74] Karnow, Stanley, *Vietnam: A History*, (Middlesex: Penguin, 1984), p.225

[75] Davies, Nick, 'Vietnam 40 Years On: How a Communist Victory Gave Way to Capitalist Corruption', *The Guardian,* 2015, Available at < https://www.theguardian.com/news/2015/apr/22/vietnam-40-years-on-how-communist-victory-gave-way-to-capitalist-corruption> , [Accessed on 1 Oct 2017]

[76] Karnow, Stanley, *Vietnam: A History*, (Middlesex: Penguin, 1984), p.225

[77] Goscha, Christopher, 'The 30-Years War in Vietnam', *The New York Times*, 2017, Available at <https://www.nytimes.com/2017/02/07/opinion/the-30-years-war-in-vietnam.html> , [Accessed on 1 Oct 2017]

[78] Ibid.

[79] Karnow, Stanley, *Vietnam: A History*, (Middlesex: Penguin, 1984), p.227

[80] Ibid. p.231

[81] Ibid. pp.234-235

[82] Ibid. p.238

[83] Ibid. p.679

[84] Ibid. p.238

⁸⁵ Ibid. p.233

⁸⁶ Goscha, Christopher, 'The 30-Years War in Vietnam', *The New York Times*, 2017, Available at <https://www.nytimes.com/2017/02/07/opinion/the-30-years-war-in-vietnam.html> , [Accessed on 1 Oct 2017]

⁸⁷ Ibid.

⁸⁸ Elliott, Mai, *RAND in Southeast Asia*, (USA: RAND Corporation: 2010), p.14

⁸⁹ Karnow, Stanley, *Vietnam: A History*, (Middlesex: Penguin, 1984), p.237

⁹⁰ Ibid. p,235

⁹¹ Ibid. p.236

⁹² Mackay, Scott, 'Scott Mackay Commentary: What Would Have Happened in Vietnam Had Kennedy Lived', *Rhode Island Public Radio,* 2017, Available at < http://ripr.org/post/scott-mackay-commentary-what-would-have-happened-vietnam-had-kennedy-lived#stream/0> , [Accessed on 4 Oct 2017]

⁹³ Karnow, Stanley, *Vietnam: A History*, (Middlesex: Penguin, 1984), p.247

⁹⁴ Ibid. p.250

⁹⁵ Ibid. p.251

⁹⁶ Ibid. p.252

⁹⁷ Ibid. p.253

⁹⁸ Ibid.

⁹⁹ Ibid. p.256

¹⁰⁰ Ibid. p.257

¹⁰¹ Mackay, Scott, 'Scott Mackay Commentary: What Would Have Happened in Vietnam Had Kennedy Lived', *Rhode Island Public Radio,* 2017, Available at < http://ripr.org/post/scott-mackay-commentary-what-would-have-happened-vietnam-had-kennedy-lived#stream/0> , [Accessed on 4 Oct 2017]

[102] Bostdorff, Denise M., and Goldzwig, Steven R., 'Idealism and Pragmatism in American Foreign Policy Rhetoric: The Case of John F. Kennedy and Vietnam', *Presidential Studies Quarterly*, 24, 3, (1994), p.519

[103] Guan, Ang Chen, 'The Vietnam War, 1962-1964: The Vietnamese Communist Perspective', *Journal of Contemporary History*, 35, 4, (2000), p.604

[104] Guan, Ang Chen, 'The Vietnam War, 1962-1964: The Vietnamese Communist Perspective', *Journal of Contemporary History*, 35, 4, (2000), p.606

[105] Karnow, Stanley, *Vietnam: A History*, (Middlesex: Penguin, 1984), p.259

[106] Karnow, Stanley, *Vietnam: A History*, (Middlesex: Penguin, 1984), p.260

[107] Guan, Ang Chen, 'The Vietnam War, 1962-1964: The Vietnamese Communist Perspective', *Journal of Contemporary History*, 35, 4, (2000), p.607

[108] Karnow, Stanley, *Vietnam: A History*, (Middlesex: Penguin, 1984), p.261

[109] Ibid.

[110] Ibid. p.262

[111] Ibid.

[112] Guan, Ang Chen, 'The Vietnam War, 1962-1964: The Vietnamese Communist Perspective', *Journal of Contemporary History*, 35, 4, (2000), p.608

[113] Karnow, Stanley, *Vietnam: A History*, (Middlesex: Penguin, 1984), p.263

[114] Ibid. p.267

[115] Ibid. p.268

[116] Ibid. p.279

[117] Ibid. p.280

[118] Ibid. p.281

[119] Ibid.

[120] Stein, Jeff, 'Death of a President', *Newsweek*, 2013, Available at <http://www.newsweek.com/2013/10/18/death-president-243702.html>, [Accessed on 12 Oct 2017]

[121] Karnow, Stanley, *Vietnam: A History*, (Middlesex: Penguin, 1984), p.310

[122] Oldweiler, Cory, 'New York Historical Society Examines the Vietnam War in New Exhibition', *New York AM*, (2017), Available at < http://www.amny.com/things-to-do/new-york-historical-society-examines-the-vietnam-war-in-new-exhibition-1.14361629>, [Accessed on 12 Oct 2017]

[123] Guan, Ang Chen, 'The Vietnam War, 1962-1964: The Vietnamese Communist Perspective', *Journal of Contemporary History*, 35, 4, (2000), p.612

[124] Peterson, Pat, 'The Truth About Tonkin', *Naval History Magazine*, 22, 1, (2008), Available at < https://www.usni.org/magazines/navalhistory/2008-02/truth-about-tonkin>, [Accessed on 15 Oct 2017]

[125] Ibid.

[126] Ibid.

[127] Ibid.

[128] Ibid.

[129] Stockdale, Jim and Sybil, *In Love and War*, (Annapolis: Naval Institute Press, 1990), p.25

[130] Peterson, Pat, 'The Truth About Tonkin', *Naval History Magazine*, 22, 1, (2008), Available at < https://www.usni.org/magazines/navalhistory/2008-02/truth-about-tonkin>, [Accessed on 15 Oct 2017]

[131] Karnow, Stanley, *Vietnam: A History*, (Middlesex: Penguin, 1984), p.377

[132] Guan, Ang Chen, 'The Vietnam War, 1962-1964: The Vietnamese Communist Perspective', *Journal of Contemporary History*, 35, 4, (2000), p.617

[133] Ibid.

[134] Karnow, Stanley, *Vietnam: A History*, (Middlesex: Penguin, 1984), p.395

[135] Drew, Col. Dennis M., *Rolling Thunder 1965: Anatomy of a Failure*, 1986, Available at <http://www.au.af.mil/au/awc/awcgate/readings/drew2.htm>, [Accessed on 17 Oct 2017]

[136] Karnow, Stanley, *Vietnam: A History*, (Middlesex: Penguin, 1984), p.402

[137] Ibid. P.409

[138] Kearns, Doris, *Lyndon Johnson and the American Dream*, (New York: Harper and Row Publishers, 1976), pp.264-265

[139] Karnow, Stanley, *Vietnam: A History*, (Middlesex: Penguin, 1984), p.409

[140] Drew, Col. Dennis M., *Rolling Thunder 1965: Anatomy of a Failure*, 1986, Available at <http://www.au.af.mil/au/awc/awcgate/readings/drew2.htm>, [Accessed on 17 Oct 2017]

[141] Littauer, Ralph and Uphoff, Norman, eds, *The Air War in Indochina*, (Boston: Beacon Press, 1972), p.37

[142] Morrocco, John, *Thunder From Above*, (Boston: Boston Publishing Company, 1984), p.56

[143] Drew, Col. Dennis M., *Rolling Thunder 1965: Anatomy of a Failure*, 1986, Available at <http://www.au.af.mil/au/awc/awcgate/readings/drew2.htm>, [Accessed on 17 Oct 2017]

[144] Jian, Chen, 'China's Involvement in the Vietnam War, 1964-69', *The China Quarterly*, 142, (1995), p.372

[145] Karnow, Stanley, *Vietnam: A History*, (Middlesex: Penguin, 1984), p.402

[146] Ibid. p.415

[147] Perera, John-Henry, '52 years ago American combat troops landed in Vietnam for the first time', *Chron*, 2017, Available at < http://www.chron.com/news/nation-world/article/52-years-ago-American-combat-troops-landed-in-10986190.php>, [Accessed on 17 Oct 2017]

[148] Karnow, Stanley, *Vietnam: A History*, (Middlesex: Penguin, 1984), p.419

[149] Ibid. P.422

[150] Asher, Glen, 'America's Rationale for Going to War with Vietnam', *Oye! Times*, 2017, Available at <http://www.oyetimes.com/views/columns/189586-americas-rationale-going-war-vietnam> , [Accessed on 19 Oct 2017]

[151] Drew, Col. Dennis M., *Rolling Thunder 1965: Anatomy of a Failure*, 1986, Available at <http://www.au.af.mil/au/awc/awcgate/readings/drew2.htm> , [Accessed on 17 Oct 2017]

[152] Karnow, Stanley, *Vietnam: A History*, (Middlesex: Penguin, 1984), p.439

[153] Ibid. p.436

[154] Ibid. p.438

[155] Warren, James A., 'How the Battle of Ia Drang Valley Changed the Course of the Vietnam War', *The Daily Beast*, 2015, Available at <https://www.thedailybeast.com/how-the-battle-of-the-ia-drang-valley-changed-the-course-of-the-vietnam-war> , [Accessed on 19 Oct 2017]

[156] Ibid.

[157] Ibid.

[158] Tracy, Jim, 'Vietnam Documentary a Compelling Look at War', *Times Union*, 2017, Available at <http://www.timesunion.com/opinion/article/Vietnam-documentary-a-compelling-look-at-war-12277513.php> , [Accesed on 19 Oct 2017]

[159] Galloway, Joseph, 'Ia Drang- The Battle that Convinced Ho Chi Minh he Could Win', *History Net*, 2010, Available at <http://www.historynet.com/ia-drang-where-battlefield-losses-convinced-ho-giap-and-mcnamara-the-u-s-could-never-win.htm> , [Accessed on 20 Oct 2017]

[160] Ibid.

[161] Ibid.

[162] Karnow, Stanley, *Vietnam: A History*, (Middlesex: Penguin, 1984), p.481

[163] Drew, Col. Dennis M., *Rolling Thunder 1965: Anatomy of a Failure*, 1986, Available at <http://www.au.af.mil/au/awc/awcgate/readings/drew2.htm> , [Accessed on 17 Oct 2017]

[164] Karnow, Stanley, *Vietnam: A History*, (Middlesex: Penguin, 1984), p.482-3

[165] Galloway, Joseph, 'Ia Drang- The Battle that Convinced Ho Chi Minh he Could Win', *History Net*, 2010, Available at <http://www.historynet.com/ia-drang-where-battlefield-losses-convinced-ho-giap-and-mcnamara-the-u-s-could-never-win.htm> , [Accessed on 20 Oct 2017]

[166] Milam, Ron, 'The Era of Big Battles in Vietnam', *The New York Times*, 2017, Available at <https://www.nytimes.com/2017/01/10/opinion/1967-the-era-of-big-battles-in-vietnam.html> , [Accessed on 21 Oct 2017]

[167] Karnow, Stanley, *Vietnam: A History*, (Middlesex: Penguin, 1984), p.503

[168] Ibid. p.500

[169] Ibid. p.502

[170] Ibid. p.505

[171] Steward Foley, Michael, 'The Moral Case for Draft Resistance', *The New York Times,* 2017, Available at <https://www.nytimes.com/2017/10/17/opinion/vietnam-draft-resistance.html> , [Accessed on 23 Oct 2017]

[172] Herring, George C., 'The Road to Tet', *The New York Times*, 2017, Available at < https://www.nytimes.com/2017/01/27/opinion/the-road-to-tet.html> [Accessed on 23 Oct 2017]

[173] Herring, George C., 'The Road to Tet', *The New York Times*, 2017, Available at < https://www.nytimes.com/2017/01/27/opinion/the-road-to-tet.html> [Accessed on 23 Oct 2017]

[174] Oberdorfer, Don, 'Tet: Who Won?', *Smithsonian Magazine,* 2004, Available at < https://www.smithsonianmag.com/history/tet-who-won-99179501/> , [Accessed on 23 Oct 2017]

[175] Karnow, Stanley, *Vietnam: A History*, (Middlesex: Penguin, 1984), p.512

[176] Oberdorfer, Don, 'Tet: Who Won?', *Smithsonian Magazine,* 2004, Available at < https://www.smithsonianmag.com/history/tet-who-won-99179501/> , [Accessed on 23 Oct 2017]

[177] Ibid.

[178] Karnow, Stanley, *Vietnam: A History*, (Middlesex: Penguin, 1984), p.544

[179] Ibid. p.525

[180] Oberdorfer, Don, 'Tet: Who Won?', *Smithsonian Magazine,* 2004, Available at < https://www.smithsonianmag.com/history/tet-who-won-99179501/> , [Accessed on 23 Oct 2017]

[181] Oberdorfer, Don, 'Tet: Who Won?', *Smithsonian Magazine,* 2004, Available at < https://www.smithsonianmag.com/history/tet-who-won-99179501/> , [Accessed on 23 Oct 2017]

[182] Karnow, Stanley, *Vietnam: A History*, (Middlesex: Penguin, 1984), p.534

[183] Ibid. p.542

[184] Atlas, Steve, 'The Tet Offensive Shocked the Nation and Permanently Changed US Attitudes Toward the Vietnam War', *PRI*, 2017, Available at <https://www.pri.org/stories/2017-10-11/tet-offensive-shocked-nation-and-permanently-changed-us-attitudes-toward-vietnam> , [Accessed on 25 Oct 2017]

[185] Karnow, Stanley, *Vietnam: A History*, (Middlesex: Penguin, 1984), p.535

[186] Oberdorfer, Don, 'Tet: Who Won?', *Smithsonian Magazine,* 2004, Available at < https://www.smithsonianmag.com/history/tet-who-won-99179501/> , [Accessed on 23 Oct 2017]

[187] Atlas, Steve, 'The Tet Offensive Shocked the Nation and Permanently Changed US Attitudes Toward the Vietnam War', *PRI*, 2017, Available at <https://www.pri.org/stories/2017-10-11/tet-offensive-shocked-nation-and-permanently-changed-us-attitudes-toward-vietnam> , [Accessed on 25 Oct 2017]

[188] Karnow, Stanley, *Vietnam: A History*, (Middlesex: Penguin, 1984), p.538

[189] Farrell, John A., 'Nixon's Vietnam Treachery', *The New York Times*, 2016, Available at <https://www.nytimes.com/2016/12/31/opinion/sunday/nixons-vietnam-treachery.html> , Accessed on [Accessed on 26 Oct 2017]

[190] Ibid.

[191] Ibid.

[192] Schultz, Colin, 'Nixon Prolongued Vietnam War for Political Gain- And Johnson Knew About it, Newly Unclassified Tapes Suggest', *Smithsonian Magazine*, 2013, Available at < https://www.smithsonianmag.com/smart-news/nixon-prolonged-vietnam-war-for-political-gainand-johnson-knew-about-it-newly-unclassified-tapes-suggest-3595441/>, [Accessed on 26 Oct 2017]

[193] Grandin, Greg, 'Henry Kissinger's Genocidal Legacy: Vietam, Cambodia and the Birth of American Militarism', *Salon*, 2015, Available at < https://www.salon.com/2015/11/10/henry_kissingers_genocidal_legacy_partner/> , [Accessed on 26 Oct 2017]

[194] Ibid.

[195] Kimball, Jeffrey, 'The Nixon Doctrine: a Saga of Misunderstanding', *Presidential Studies Quarterly*, 36, 1, 2006, p.59

[196] Ibid, p.60

[197] Karnow, Stanley, *Vietnam: A History*, (Middlesex: Penguin, 1984), p.582

[198] Ibid. p.593

[199] Suri, Jeremi, 'Donald Trump and the Madman Playbook', *Wired*, 2017, Available at <https://www.wired.com/story/donald-trump-madman-strategy-north-korea-nuclear-weapons/> , [Accessed on 30 Oct 2017]

[200] Karnow, Stanley, *Vietnam: A History*, (Middlesex: Penguin, 1984), p.595

[201] Ibid.

[202] Ibid. p.597

[203] Friedman, Ian C., 'The Great Silent Majority', *Words Matter*, 2010, Available at <http://www.iancfriedman.com/?p=1134> , [Accessed on 29 Oct 2017]

204 Karnow, Stanley, *Vietnam: A History*, (Middlesex: Penguin, 1984), p.599

205 Friedman, Ian C., 'The Great Silent Majority', *Words Matter*, 2010, Available at <http://www.iancfriedman.com/?p=1134> , [Accessed on 29 Oct 2017]

206 Editorial, 'My Lai Revisited: 47 Years Later, Seymour Hersh Travels to Vietnam Site of U.S. Massacre he Exposed', *Democracy Now*, 2015, Available at < https://www.democracynow.org/2015/3/25/my_lai_revisited_47_years_later> , [Accessed on 29 Oct 2017]

207 Hersh, Seymour M., 'The Scene of the Crime', *The New Yorker*, 2015, Available at < https://www.newyorker.com/magazine/2015/03/30/the-scene-of-the-crime> , [Accessed on 29 Oct 2017]

208 Ibid.

209 Ibid.

210 Ibid.

211 Fifield, Russel H., 'The Thirty Years War in Indochina: A Conceptual Framework'. *Asian Survey*, 17, 9, 1977, p.866

212 Friedman, Ian C., 'The Great Silent Majority', *Words Matter*, 2010, Available at <http://www.iancfriedman.com/?p=1134> , [Accessed on 29 Oct 2017]

213 Karnow, Stanley, *Vietnam: A History*, (Middlesex: Penguin, 1984), pp.623-24

214 Ibid. p.624

215 Editorial, 'A Peace that Couldn't Last- Negotiating the Paris Accords on Vietnam', *Association for Diplomatic Studies and Training*, 2016, Available at <http://adst.org/2016/01/a-peace-that-couldnt-last-negotiating-the-paris-accords-on-vietnam/#.WfpnuWi0PIW> , [Accessed on 01 Nov 2017]

216 Karnow, Stanley, *Vietnam: A History*, (Middlesex: Penguin, 1984), pp.625

217 Ibid. p.630

218 Ibid.

219 Ibid. p.626

220 Hess, Gary R., 'The Unending Debate: Historians and the Vietnam War', *Diplomatic History*, 18, 2, 1994, p.240

221 Karnow, Stanley, *Vietnam: A History*, (Middlesex: Penguin, 1984), pp.631

222 Editorial, 'Bad Blood: The Sino-Soviet Split and the U.S. Normalization with China', *Association for Diplomatic Studies and Training*, 2016, Available at <http://adst.org/2016/08/bad-blood-sino-soviet-split-u-s-normalization-china/#.Wfpgnmi0PIU> , [Accessed on 01 Nov 2017]

223 Ibid. p.638

224 Fifield, Russel H., 'The Thirty Years War in Indochina: A Conceptual Framework'. *Asian Survey*, 17, 9, 1977, p.868

225 Editorial, 'A Peace that Couldn't Last- Negotiating the Paris Accords on Vietnam', *Association for Diplomatic Studies and Training*, 2016, Available at <http://adst.org/2016/01/a-peace-that-couldnt-last-negotiating-the-paris-accords-on-vietnam/#.WfpnuWi0PIW> , [Accessed on 01 Nov 2017]

226 Ibid.

227 Ibid.

228 Ibid.

229 Ibid.

230 Fifield, Russel H., 'The Thirty Years War in Indochina: A Conceptual Framework'. *Asian Survey*, 17, 9, 1977, p.869

231 Editorial, 'A Peace that Couldn't Last- Negotiating the Paris Accords on Vietnam', *Association for Diplomatic Studies and Training*, 2016, Available at <http://adst.org/2016/01/a-peace-that-couldnt-last-negotiating-the-paris-accords-on-vietnam/#.WfpnuWi0PIW> , [Accessed on 01 Nov 2017]

232 Fifield, Russel H., 'The Thirty Years War in Indochina: A Conceptual Framework'. *Asian Survey*, 17, 9, 1977, p.865

233 Karnow, Stanley, *Vietnam: A History*, (Middlesex: Penguin, 1984), pp.686

[234] Editorial, 'A Peace that Couldn't Last- Negotiating the Paris Accords on Vietnam', *Association for Diplomatic Studies and Training*, 2016, Available at <http://adst.org/2016/01/a-peace-that-couldnt-last-negotiating-the-paris-accords-on-vietnam/#.WfpnuWi0PIW> , [Accessed on 01 Nov 2017]

[235] Ibid.

[236] Karnow, Stanley, *Vietnam: A History*, (Middlesex: Penguin, 1984), pp.687

[237] Fifield, Russel H., 'The Thirty Years War in Indochina: A Conceptual Framework'. *Asian Survey*, 17, 9, 1977, p.865

ABOUT CAPTIVATING HISTORY

A lot of history books just contain dry facts that will eventually bore the reader. That's why Captivating History was created. Now you can enjoy history books that will mesmerize you. But be careful though, hours can fly by, and before you know it; you're up reading way past bedtime.

Get your first history book for free here:
http://www.captivatinghistory.com/ebook

Make sure to follow us on Twitter: @CaptivHistory
and Facebook: www.facebook.com/captivatinghistory so you can get all of our updates!

Printed in Great Britain
by Amazon